The Origins of the Canons of Hippolytus

Nathan P. Chase

Maxwell E. Johnson

LITURGICAL PRESS
ACADEMIC

Collegeville, Minnesota
litpress.org

Library of Congress Cataloging-in-Publication Data

Names: Chase, Nathan, author. | Johnson, Maxwell E., 1952– author.
Title: The origins of the Canons of Hippolytus / Nathan P. Chase, Maxwell E. Johnson.
Description: Collegeville, Minnesota : Liturgical Press Academic, [2024] | Includes bibliographical references. | Summary: "Can a case still be made for Egyptian origin of the Canons of Hippolytus? This is the question that Maxwell E. Johnson and Nathan P. Chase focus on in response to the recent translation of and commentary on the Canons of Hippolytus by Alistair Stewart, who claims a Cappadocian origin, with a possibly later Egyptian redaction. In The Origins of the Canons of Hippolytus, the authors look at the relevant canons and argue for an Egyptian origin, supporting the claim that the Canons of Hippolytus remain the earliest derivative document of the Apostolic tradition"— Provided by publisher.
Identifiers: LCCN 2024024914 (print) | LCCN 2024024915 (ebook) | ISBN 9780814689158 (trade paperback) | ISBN 9780814689165 (epub) | ISBN 9780814689172 (pdf)
Subjects: LCSH: Canon law—Early church, ca. 30-600. | Church orders, Ancient. | Sacramentaries. | Liturgies, Early Christian. | Hippolytus, Antipope, approximately 170-235 or 236.
Classification: LCC KBR196.22 .C43 2024 (print) | LCC KBR196.22 (ebook) | DDC 262.9/22—dc23/eng/20240819
LC record available at https://lccn.loc.gov/2024024914
LC ebook record available at https://lccn.loc.gov/2024024915

"This work provides us with a significant advance in our understanding and knowledge of an important fourth-century church order, and to some extent of its principal source, *The Apostolic Tradition*. A substantial introduction is followed by a revised English translation of the text and a comprehensive commentary that takes account of all the relevant parallels in the literature of the period. This will make it invaluable to all those interested in the development of early Christian life."

> —Paul F. Bradshaw, emeritus professor of liturgy,
> University of Notre Dame

"The primary aim of this book is to revisit Alistair C. Stewart's claim about an Asian or Antiochene layer in the *Canons of Hippolytus* and to argue for the traditional view, that this derivative of *The Apostolic Tradition* was compiled in Egypt. Nathan Chase and Maxwell Johnson argue this convincingly, but they also offer the reader much more. They bring us a detailed study of the material proper to the *Canons of Hipploytus*, and through comparison with an impressive variety of sources, they illuminate several aspects of Egyptian liturgy in the fourth century."

> —Ágnes T. Mihálykó, St. Athanasius Greek Catholic
> Theological Institute, Hungary

"In the many iterations of the so-called *Apostolic Tradition*, the *Canons of Hippolytus* is an important early example. Drawing on the Ethiopian evidence of the Aksumite Collection, Nathan Chase and Maxwell Johnson present a well-argued and convincing case for accepting Egypt as the sole provenance of this Church Order. This work is crucial for all who study liturgy and ministry in early Christian Egypt."

> —Bryan D. Spinks, Bishop F. Percy Goddard Professor
> Emeritus of Liturgical Studies and Pastoral Theology,
> Yale Institute of Sacred Music and Yale Divinity School

Contents

Commentary

Abbreviations

ACO	*Apostolic Church Order*
ANF	The Ante-Nicene Fathers
ApCons	*Apostolic Constitutions*
ApTrad	*The Apostolic Tradition*
BR-AC	Baptismal Ritual in the Aksumite Collection
CA	*Canons of Athanasius*
CB	*Canons of Basil*
CH	*Canons of Hippolytus*
CSCO	Corpus Scriptorum Christianorum Orientalium
Ethio-MC	The Ethiopian Mystagogical Catechesis
Euch-AC	Euchologion in the Aksumite Collection
GCN	*Gnomai of the Council of Nicaea*
GCS	Die Griechischen Christlichen Schriftsteller der ersten Jahrhunderte
Herm. Com. 2002	*The Apostolic Tradition: A Commentary*
MARK	The Anaphora of St. Mark
OCP	*Orientalia Christiana Periodica*
SD	*Syntagma Doctrinae*
TD	*Testamentum Domini*

Introduction

In his recent book on the *Canons of Hippolytus* (CH),[1] Alistair C. Stewart has sought to reopen discussions on the provenance of this important derivative of *The Apostolic Tradition* (ApTrad).[2] While seeing the document as mid-fourth century in origin,[3] Stewart has tentatively suggested that there are two redactional layers in the text. The first is an older "Asian or Antiochene" reworking of the material contained

We would like to extend a special thanks to the "Problems in the Early History of Liturgy" seminar at the North American Academy of Liturgy where we presented an early draft of this project and received wonderful feedback. We are also grateful for Harald Buchinger's detailed feedback. We would also like to thank Monica Cronin, who served as Nathan Chase's research assistant, and Aquinas Institute for their help with and support of this project. A special thanks also to Paul Bradshaw for allowing us to reproduce the translation here.

1. Alistair Stewart, *The Canons of Hippolytus: An English Version, with Introduction and Annotation and an Accompanying Arabic Text* (Macquarie Centre: SCD Press, 2021).

2. Paul Bradshaw, Maxwell Johnson, and L. Edward Phillips, *The Apostolic Tradition: A Commentary*, Hermeneia—A Critical and Historical Commentary on the Bible (Minneapolis: Fortress Press, 2002); henceforth *Herm. Com.* 2002. See also more recently Paul F. Bradshaw, *The Apostolic Tradition Reconstructed: A Text for Students*, JLS/Joint Liturgical Studies 91 (Norwich: Alcuin Club and the Group for Renewal of Worship, 2021); Paul F. Bradshaw, *Apostolic Tradition: A New Commentary* (Collegeville, MN: Liturgical Press Academic, 2023). For a different interpretation of the document, see Alistair Stewart, *On the Apostolic Tradition* (Crestwood, NY: St. Vladimir's Seminary Press, 2015).

3. Stewart, *The Canons of Hippolytus*, 3–6 and 7–18.

in ApTrad, and the second is a lighter Egyptian editing.[4] This leads him to a dating between 340 and 380 CE, rather than the 336–340 CE traditionally ascribed to the work.[5] This study will assess Stewart's claims by focusing our attention on those particular canons which have a bearing on the question of provenance, but more broadly it will look at the relationship between ApTrad and CH in light of a new witness and new commentaries on ApTrad.

I. The Church Orders

The date and place of origin of the "church orders" is difficult to determine, since they are a form of "living literature," which consists of various redactional layers from different times and places.[6] Among the major church orders, only the *Didache,*[7] *Didascalia,*[8] and *Apostolic Constitutions* (ApCons)[9] can be safely attributed to any region, namely Syria. *Testamentum Domini* (TD)[10] and the

4. Stewart, 61–62.

5. Paul F. Bradshaw, *Ancient Church Orders*, Joint Liturgical Studies 80 (Norwich: Hymns Ancient and Modern, 2015), 18.

6. For an overview, see Bradshaw, *Ancient Church Orders*.

7. Kurt Niederwimmer and Harold W. Attridge, *The Didache: A Commentary* (Minneapolis: Fortress Press, 1998).

8. Alistair Stewart-Sykes, ed., *The Didascalia Apostolorum: An English Version*, Studia Traditionis Theologiae 1 (Turnhout: Brepols, 2009).

9. For the liturgical portions, see W. Jardine Grisbrooke, ed., *The Liturgical Portions of the Apostolic Constitutions: A Text for Students*, Alcuin/GROW Liturgical Study 13–14 (Bramcote: Grove Books, 1990).

10. For an overview, see Grant Sperry-White, *The Testamentum Domini: A Text for Students, with Introduction, Translation, and Notes* (Nottingham: Grove Books Limited, 1991). Since Sperry-White's work, there have been some new fragments: Tinatin Chronz and Heinzgerd Brakmann, "Fragmente Des *Testamentum Domini* in Georgischer Übersetzung," *Zeitschrift Für Antikes Christentum* 13 (2009): 395–402; Simon Corcoran and Benet Salway, "The

Apostolic Church Order (ACO)[11] are placed by most scholars in Syria and Egypt, respectively. At the same time, the provenance of TD is difficult to determine, especially since it also circulated in Egypt at a very early date.[12] Stewart has pushed back against this scholarly consensus and sees TD as Cappadocian[13] and the ACO as "Asian."[14] ApTrad's place

---

Newly Identified Greek Fragment of the *Testamentum Domini*," *Journal of Theological Studies* 62 (2011): 118–35. The various recensions of TD and their relationship is rather complex and in need of much further study. There are three main witnesses to this church order: the Syriac, the Ethiopic, and the Arabic, as well as a number of fragmentary witnesses in Greek (the original language), Georgian, Coptic, and Latin. The Arabic is itself divided into four separate recensions: B, L, M, and D. For an overview of the sources and provenance, see Martin Lüstraeten, "Edition und Übersetzung der Euchologie der Eucharistiefeier der Redaktion 'M' des arabischen *Testamentum Domini* (I.23-I.28)," *Ex Fonte - Journal of Ecumenical Studies in Liturgy* 2 (2023): 65–179, especially pp. 67–93; Martin Lüstraeten, "The Eucharistic Prayer in the Arabic Tradition of the Testamentum Domini," forthcoming in the proceedings from *The Eighth International Congress of the Society of Oriental Liturgy; 3–18 June, 2022, Thessaloniki, Greece.* For provenance, see also Michael Kohlbacher, "Wessen Kirche ordnete das Testamentum Domini Nostri Jesu Christi? Anmerkungen zum historischen Kontext von CPG 1743," in *Zu Geschichte, Theologie, Liturgie und Gegenwartslage der syrischen Kirchen. Ausgewählte Vorträge des deutschen Syrologen-Symposiums vom 2.-4. Oktober 1998 in Hermannsburg,* ed. Martin Tamcke and Andreas Heinz, SOKG 9 (Münster: LIT, 2000), 55–137. For an English translation, see James Cooper and Arthur John Maclean, *The Testament of Our Lord* (Edinburgh: T&T Clark, 1902).

11. Alistair Stewart-Sykes, *The Apostolic Church Order: The Greek Text with Introduction, Translation and Annotation* (Strathfield: St. Paul's Publications, Centre for Early Christian Studies, Australian Catholic University, 2006).

12. For questions of provenance, see the sources in n. 10. For the text's early circulation in Egypt, see Alessandro Bausi, "Testamentum Domini," in *Encyclopaedia Aethiopica,* ed. Siegbert Uhlig and Alessandro Bausi, vol. 4, 2010, 928.

13. Stewart, *The Canons of Hippolytus,* 37.

14. Stewart-Sykes, *The Apostolic Church Order.*

of origin remains thoroughly disputed,[15] and CH has almost universally been considered Egyptian.[16]

The major church orders also influenced a number of related texts like the *Canons of Athanasius* (CA), the *Canons of Basil* (CB), the *Syntagma Doctrinae* (SD), and the *Gnomai of the Council of Nicaea* (GCN). CA is thought to date to the end of the fourth, or the beginning of the fifth century, from Egypt,[17] though Stewart claims its provenance is "uncertain."[18] CB is a text from Syria which circulated and was reformu-

15. *Herm. Com.* 2002; Stewart, *On the Apostolic Tradition.*

16. Bradshaw, *Ancient Church Orders*, 17–18.

17. For a summary, see Ágnes T. Mihálykó, *The Christian Liturgical Papyri: An Introduction*, Studien und Texte zu Antike und Christentum 114 (Tübingen: Mohr Siebeck, 2019), 44. For a more detailed discussion, see Ewa Wipszycka, "A Certain Bishop and a Certain Diocese in Egypt at the Turn of the Fourth and Fifth Centuries: The Testimony of the Canons of Athanasius," *U Schyłku Starożytności: Studia Źródłoznawcze = Late Antiquity: Studies in Source Criticism* 17/18 (2018/2019): 91–115.

18. Stewart, *The Canons of Hippolytus*, 61.

19. Alberto Camplani and Federico Contardi, "Remarks on the Textual Contribution of the Coptic Codices preserving the Canons of Saint Basil, with Edition of the Ordination Rite for the Bishop (Canon 46)," in *Philologie, herméneutique et histoire des textes entre Orient et Occident: Mélanges en hommage à Sever J. Voicu*, ed. Francesca Prometea Barone, Caroline Macé, and Pablo Alejandro Ubierna (Turnhout: Brepols, 2017), 139–59; Mihálykó, *The Christian Liturgical Papyri*, 45. The Arabic version is published in Wilhelm Riedel, *Die Kirchenrechtsquellen des Patriarchats Alexandrien* (Leipzig: A. Deichert, nachf. G. Böhme, 1900), 278–83.

20. H. Hyvernat, "Le Syntagma Doctrinae," in *Studia Patristica: Études d'ancienne Littérature Chrétienne*, ed. Pierre Batiffol (Paris: Leroux, 1890), 118–60.

21. Alistair Stewart, ed., *The Gnomai of the Council of Nicea (CC 0021): Critical Text with Translation, Introduction and Commentary*, Texts from Christian Late Antiquity 35 (Piscataway, NJ: Gorgias Press, 2015).

lated in sixth-century Egypt.[19] The SD is from fourth-century Egypt,[20] as is the mid-fourth-century GCN.[21]

Turning to the CH, this text, as noted, is universally considered by scholars to be a derivative of ApTrad. But ApTrad itself has its own redactional layers taken from different times, contexts, and places.[22] Paul Bradshaw, Maxwell Johnson, and Edward Phillips in their 2002 commentary (henceforth *Herm. Com.* 2002) believe that the document consisted of three core sections, likely three sources of original material, that were combined together:[23]

- Directives about appointment to ministry:
  - 2.1-4; 7.1; 8.1; 9.1-2(?); 10.1-3; 11; 12*; 13; 14
- Directives about the initiation of new converts:
  - 15; 16; 17; 18; 19; 20; 21.1-5, 12-18, 20, 25-26
- Directives about community meals and prayer:
  - 23*; 24 (=29B); 25 (=29C)*; 26(?); 27; 28.4-6; 29A; 30A; 31; 32; 33; 35

The rest of the material found in ApTrad represents expansions[24] or additions[25] to this original core.

The chapters above with an asterisk (*), however, may not have been part of the original source material. With the witness of Ethiopic I (see below), there is a need to reassess the

---

22. *Herm. Com.* 2002. For an overview of the layers, see especially Bradshaw, *The Apostolic Tradition Reconstructed.* See also Bradshaw's new commentary—Bradshaw, *Apostolic Tradition.*

23. *Herm. Com.* 2002, 14–15.

24. 2.5; 7.2-5; 8.2-12; 9.2-5; 10.4-5; 21.6-11, 19, 21-24, 27-40; 28.1-3.

25. 1; 3; 4; 5; 6; 22; 29D; 30B; 34; 36; 37; 38A; 38B; 39; 40; 41; 42; 43.

earlier core of ApTrad. It is very possible that Chs. 12, 23.4, and 25 (29C.10-15) are later additions to the text, which are not in Ethiopic I and which were possibly not in the Latin version either (in these places the Latin is lacuna). Ch. 12 does not make its way into CH either, except possibly in CH 7. Ch. 29Ab is very likely a later addition since it is not contained in either the Latin or Ethiopic I sources or in any of ApTrad's derivatives. A few other chapters/verses also need to be accounted for. Ch. 7.2-5 is in the Latin and Ethiopic II and is also paralleled in ApCons and TD, but it is not in Ethiopic I or CH. Ch. 8.9-12 is in the Latin and Ethiopic II, as well as the Arabic version of the *Clementine Octateuch*,[26] but is not in Ethiopic I and is substantially different in CH 5. Ch. 35 is in all sources except Ethiopic I and CH, but this is already largely a duplication of Ch. 41.[27]

What this preliminary analysis seems to indicate with regard to CH is that CH appears to derive from a slightly earlier form of ApTrad than the received text. This may suggest that at times CH preserves older readings than even the earliest versions of ApTrad, namely the Latin and Ethiopic I witnesses. In fact, what actually constitutes ApTrad is a subject of debate, since there is, simply, no document known as ApTrad apart from the various translations (Verona Latin, now two Ethiopic versions, Sahidic/Bohairic, and Arabic), derivative documents (CH, TD, and ApCons), and fragments in which it appears.[28] For our purposes here, reference to ApTrad is to the Latin text

---

26. Reinhard Messner, "Die Angebliche *Traditio Apostolica*," *Archiv Für Liturgiewissenschaft* 58–59 (2016): 17–18 and 23–24.

27. Cf. Nathan Chase, "Another Look at the 'Daily Office' in the Apostolic Tradition," *Studia Liturgica* 49 (2019): 5–25.

28. For the correspondences between these translations and derivatives, with the exception of the new Ethiopic translation (see nn. 29 and 31), see *Herm. Com.* 2002.

and the new Ethiopic translation from the Aksumite Collection (Ethiopic I), edited and translated by Alessandro Bausi[29] and dated to the second half of the fifth century or first half of the sixth century.[30] There is strong agreement between the Latin version and Ethiopic I, reflecting either a late fourth- or early fifth-century context from which to posit a common original Greek source upon which these are based, albeit with some divergences and a different sequence of the chapters in places.[31] This is not the case with the Sahidic, Arabic, and Ethiopic II versions of ApTrad, which often are different. Here we presume the ordering of the chapters of ApTrad according to *Herm. Com.* 2002.[32] Given the strong textual agreement between the Latin and Ethiopic I versions, our comments are based on the Latin edition, which is the primary text in *Herm. Com.* 2002. Any divergences between the Latin and Ethiopic I versions will be noted, as well as instances where the Ethiopic I version supplies text missing in the Latin version. In a few cases, comparison will also be made to the Sahidic, Arabic,

---

29. Alessandro Bausi, "La 'nuova' versione ethiopica della *Traditio apostolica*: Edizione e traduzione preliminare," in *Christianity in Egypt: Literary Production and Intellectual Trends*, ed. Paola Buzi and Alberto Camplani (Rome: Institutum Patristicum Augustinianum, 2011), 21–69.

30. Alessandro Bausi and Alberto Camplani, "New Ethiopic Documents for the History of Christian Egypt," *Zeitschrift Für Antikes Christentum* 17 (2013): 217.

31. For an overview, see Alessandro Bausi, "The 'so-called *Traditio apostolica*': Preliminary observations on the new Ethiopic evidence," in *Volksglaube im antiken Christentum*, ed. Theofried Baumeister and Andreas Merkt (Darmstadt: WBG, Wissenschaftliche Buchgesellschaft, 2009), 291–321; Alessandro Bausi, "The *Baptismal Ritual* in the Earliest Ethiopic Canonical Liturgical Collection," in *"Neugeboren aus Wasser und Heiligem Geist": Kölner Kolloquium zur Initiatio Christiana*, ed. Heinzgerd Brakmann, Tinatin Chronz, and Claudia Sode (Münster: Aschendorff Verlag, 2020), 41–52.

32. *Herm. Com.* 2002. This is also the ordering used in Bradshaw, *The Apostolic Tradition Reconstructed*; Bradshaw, *Apostolic Tradition*.

and Ethiopic II versions, and this too will be noted in the commentary below.

Concerning the derivatives of the church orders, it is important to note that divergences between a derivative church order and its primary source often point to different times or places of composition, since derivative liturgical texts attempt to make the source-text relevant to the practices of a particular community.[33] Places where the source document and its derivative agree likely represent common liturgical practice, whereas changes between the source document and the derivative shed light on local practice. The derivatives also attempt to make sense of directives in the source document that are not clear. This is especially the case with CH's treatment of ApTrad's *horarium*[34] and meal practices.[35] It is also not inconceivable that in some places CH is preserving an older reading than the received witnesses of ApTrad.

II. Comparing *The Apostolic Tradition* and the *Canons of Hippolytus*

The key divergences between CH and ApTrad are listed in the table below. There are only three chapters in ApTrad that do not make their way into CH in any form:[36] ApTrad 1 (which has been replaced by CH 1); ApTrad 35 (which has parallels to ApTrad 41 and thus CH 26–27); and ApTrad 43. This essentially means that the framing of CH has been changed, but the content of ApTrad has been almost entirely taken over

33. Stewart, *The Canons of Hippolytus*, 16–17 and 45.

34. Chase, "Another Look," 18.

35. Stewart, *The Canons of Hippolytus*, 57–60.

36. CH 7 may incorporate parts of ApTrad 12, but otherwise this chapter in ApTrad is also not carried over into CH.

into CH even if it has been thoroughly reorganized in places.[37] Divisions of canons into a, b, c, etc., can be found in the commentary below as well as in the table in some special cases.

CH, canon #	ApTrad, chapter #	Comments
1		CH is a new creation. Some thematic similarity to ApTrad 1 (also 30B).
2	2	CH adapts ApTrad.
3a	3	CH adapts ApTrad.
3b	4	CH adapts ApTrad but omits the anaphora.
3c	5; 6; 31/32	CH omits all the prayers and conflates ApTrad 5 and 6 with ApTrad 31/32.
4	7	CH is different from ApTrad, ApCons, and TD.
5	8 (also 29B and 34)	CH interweaves multiple texts of ApTrad (8, 29B, 34) and is similar to TD; the prayer is based on similar themes as those in ApTrad and TD, while being different.
6	9	CH reworks ApTrad.
7	11, 12, and 13	CH adds to the reader "to have virtue of deacon" (specific virtues are given in TD). CH also conflates ApTrad 11, 12, and 13, though differently from TD.

37. While CH seems to replace ApTrad 34 and 35 with Chs. 39–41, the location of that block of material in CH is in a very different place. The corresponding canons in CH (e.g., 24–27) are out of place. They have been shifted up in the document and are placed after initiation (CH 19 = ApTrad 21) and before the instructions on the importance of caring for the bread and wine and fasting practices (CH 28 = ApTrad 36, 37, and 38A). These latter instructions have also been moved up before the discussion of communion more broadly (CH 30 = ApTrad 22). Thus, CH seems to have transposed a number of sections taken over from ApTrad.

CH, canon #	ApTrad, chapter #	Comments
8	14	CH is based on ApTrad 14, but adds a note about presbyters.
9a		CH is a new creation.
9b	10	CH simplifies ApTrad 10.
10	15	CH simplifies ApTrad 15.
11	16.3	CH is based on ApTrad 16.3, but adds a note about readmission if they create images or idols after their baptism.
12	16–17	CH modifies ApTrad 16–17. The second half of CH is a new creation.
13	16.9-11	CH is based on ApTrad 16.9-11, but adds a note that the bishop is not to pray with unrighteous magistrates.
14	16.11	CH adapts ApTrad.
15a	16.12-14	CH is adapted from ApTrad 16.12-14.
15b[38]		CH is a new creation.
16	16.15-17	CH shifts this canon to a Christian with a concubine rather than a catechumen as in ApTrad.
17a		CH is largely a new creation.
17b	17	CH is largely an adaptation of ApTrad.
18	18–19.1	CH expands ApTrad.
19a[39]		CH is a new creation.
19b[40]	20	CH expands ApTrad 20.2 and omits ApTrad 20.3-4 and 20.10.

38. This begins at "and three witnesses have testified . . . ."

39. This is the opening material of CH 19 before the heading "Chapter of the Catechumens."

40. This is the material in the "Chapter of the Catechumens" up to the paragraph that begins: "On the Saturday/the seventh day of the week the bishop assembles . . . ."

CH, canon #	ApTrad, chapter #	Comments
19c[41]	21	CH has slightly different instructions from ApTrad 21.7-8; CH adds a turn to the West in the renunciation; CH adds a turn to the East for the *syntaxis* and also omits the role of the bishop; CH adds a *syntaxis* formula; CH adds the indicative formula; CH changes episcopal post-baptismal anointing; CH omits the anointing formula in ApTrad 21.22; CH abbreviates ApTrad 21.27; CH merges and adapts ApTrad 21.28 with 21.33a, while omitting the rest of this passage and creating new distribution formulas.
19d[42]		CH is a new creation based on ApTrad 21.38 and ApTrad 29A.
19e[43]	33 and 36	CH adapts ApTrad 33 and 36.
19f[44]	36	CH adapts from ApTrad 36. Parallels also possible to ApTrad 26 and 33. The reference to the assembly of catechumens parallels ApTrad 15, 17-19, and 20 (especially verse 7).
20a		CH is a new creation.
20b	26 and 28.5	CH is based on ApTrad 26 and 28.5 (also 29D).

41. This section begins with the paragraph "On the Saturday/the seventh day of the week the bishop assembles" and concludes with the paragraph that ends, "which does not return to bitterness and does not fade away."

42. The paragraph "Thus they have become complete Christians . . . and better than the common behaviour of people."

43. The paragraph "As for those who have been baptized . . . he can eat what he wishes."

44. The paragraph "All the catechumens are to assemble . . . received the body and the blood."

CH, canon #	ApTrad, chapter #	Comments
21a		New creation, but this is an expansion of the morning assemblies referenced in ApTrad 18, 19, 35, 39, and 41.
21b		CH is a new creation.
22	33	First part is new in CH. The remainder is from ApTrad 33.
23		CH is a new creation.
24	34 and 39	CH adapts ApTrad.
25a	40.2	CH adapts ApTrad.
25b	41.1, 5-10, and 11	CH thoroughly simplifies and adapts ApTrad 41 (also ApTrad 35).
26-27	41	CH is similar to ApTrad.
28	36–37	CH simplifies ApTrad and modifies it to the liturgy.
29a	37 and 38A	CH adapts ApTrad 37 and 38A.
29b		CH is a new creation.
29c	38B and 42	CH adapts ApTrad 38B and 42. Possibly also ApTrad 21.38-39.
30	21.40; 22; 24 (=29B)	CH adapts ApTrad.
31		CH is a new creation, but rooted in references in ApTrad 21.33; 22; 28.5; 29D.
32	23; 24 (=29B); 25 (=29C)	CH adapts ApTrad.

CH, canon #	ApTrad, chapter #	Comments
33	26.2; 27; 28.1-2	CH adapts ApTrad.
34	28.3-5 (=29D)	CH adapts ApTrad.
35	28.5-6 (=29D); 29A; 30A	CH adapts ApTrad.
36	31–32	Quite different from ApTrad, but its prayer is similar to the prayer in TD.
37		CH is a new creation.
38		CH is a new creation.

As noted above, in the following, only those differences between ApTrad and CH that have a possible bearing on the provenance of CH will be discussed below in detail.

Commentary

CH §1[1]

Concerning the Holy Faith

Before all else we speak of the holy and true faith in our Lord Jesus Christ, Son of the living God. We have set it down faithfully, and we are firmly in agreement [with it], and we say that the Trinity, equal and perfect in honor, is equal in glory. He has no beginning or end, the Word, the Son of God, and he is also the creator of every creature, visible and invisible. This we have set down and we truly agree with it.

As for those who have dared to say what they should not about the Word of God, according to what our Lord Jesus Christ said concerning them, we have assembled ourselves, being the great majority, in the power of God, and we have cut them off because they are not in accord with the holy Scriptures, the word of God, or with us, the disciples of the Scriptures. That is why we have cut them off from the Church, and we have handed over their case to God, who judges every creature with justice.

Those who do not know these things, we teach them without ill-will, so that they may not fall into a bad death, as some heretics, but may be worthy of eternal life, and teach their children and those who will come after them this holy faith.

1. The English translation of the canons quoted throughout this commentary has been adapted and occasionally corrected or edited from Paul F. Bradshaw, ed., *The Canons of Hippolytus*, Alcuin/GROW Liturgical Study 2 (Bramcote: Grove Books, 1987). Used with Paul Bradshaw's permission.

This canon is a new creation in CH that does not have a direct textual parallel, though the beginning statement of faith does find support in CB and SD.[2] There are also some thematic similarities to ApTrad 1 (and by extension ApTrad 30B). The canon clearly has a Trinitarian and Nicene focus. It also reveals tensions in the community using this text. There are clear doctrinal disputes with some in the local church holding to heretical views on the Son of God in particular. Stewart notes that the phrase "the Son of God, and he is also the creator of every creature, visible and invisible" parallels Colossians 1:16 and a number of Asian creeds.[3] However, Christ's role in creation is also a very important hallmark of Egyptian anaphoras in this period and so this emphasis cannot automatically be assumed to be Cappadocian.[4] Furthermore, there are some thematic parallels to the Egyptian treatise "On the One Judge" contained in the Aksumite Collection.[5]

2. Bradshaw, 11n1; Stewart, *The Canons of Hippolytus*, 23.

3. Stewart, *The Canons of Hippolytus*, 73n14.

4. Nathan P. Chase, *The Anaphoral Tradition in the "Barcelona Papyrus,"* Studia Traditionis Theologiae 53 (Turnhout: Brepols, 2023), Chs. 6 and 7.

5. Alessandro Bausi, "The Treatise *On the One Judge* (CAe 6260) in the *Aksumite Collection* (CAe1047)," *Adamantius* 27 (2021): 215–56. This is also paralleled in the Egyptian anaphoras; see *in passim* Chase, *The Anaphoral Tradition*.

CH §2

Concerning Bishops

Let the bishop be chosen by all the people, and let him be without reproach, as it is written concerning him in the Apostle. The week when he is ordained, all the clergy and the people say, 'We choose him.' There shall be silence in all the flock after the confession, and they are all to pray for him and say, 'O God, look upon him whom you have prepared for us.' They are to choose one of the bishops and presbyters; he lays his hand on the head and prays, saying . . .

This canon is adapted from the relevant section of ApTrad 2, as is much of the ordination material in CH.[1] The text diverges from ApTrad in seeming to allow for both a bishop and presbyter to take part in the handlaying ritual rather than just one bishop as in ApTrad 2.5. Stewart suggests that this could be the result of "a redactor familiar with presbyteral ordination of the *episkopos*, faced with a text enforcing episcopal

1. Heinzgerd Brakmann, "Pseudoapostolische Ordinationsgebete in apostolischen Kirchen. Beobachtungen zur gottesdienstlichen Rezeption der Traditio Apostolica und ihrer Deszendenten," in *Liturgies in East and West: Ecumenical Relevance of Early Liturgical Development. Acts of the International Symposium Vindobonnense I, Vienna, November 17–20, 2007,* ed. Hans-Jürgen Feulner, Österreichische Studien zur Liturgiewissenschaft und Sakramententheologie 6 (Vienna: LIT, 2013), 66–67.

ordination of the *episkopos*, expand[ing] the text in order to embrace the continued involvement of the presbyterate."[2] He has suggested either Egyptian or Cappadocian "backwaters" as possible places, since this document seems to suggest the relatively recent emergence of the monepiscopate.[3] While his first comment seems correct, there is no need for this to have been in an Egyptian backwater, at least based on this inclusion, since presbyters in Egypt were closely involved in the ordination process of their bishops. The reference to the ordination occurring "on the Sabbath" in CH has parallels in both Egypt and Asia.[4] There are also parallels here between CH and CA canons 14–16 (Arabic),[5] which, like CH, also interpret the office of the bishop primarily as one of service.

What is known about ordinations in the early Egyptian sources has to be pieced together from brief accounts and liturgical prayers like that in the sacramentary of Sarapion of Thmuis. Other sources that specify the process in more detail, like CB 46, are thought to be non-Egyptian in origin (more below).[6] In fact, besides CH, CB, and the sacramentary of Sarapion of Thmuis, there is only one other text that may refer to the ordination ritual of a bishop in this period: P.Ryl.Copt. 23, which is from Hermopolis and dated to the

2. Stewart, *The Canons of Hippolytus*, 45–46.

3. Stewart, 37–38 and 45–46.

4. Stewart, 42 and 75n18; Ewa Wipszycka, *The Alexandrian Church: People and Institutions*, The Journal of Juristic Papyrology Supplement 25 (Warsaw: Faculty of Law and Administration of the University of Warsaw, 2015), 132.

5. Wilhelm Riedel and W. E. Crum, *The Canons of Athanasius of Alexandria: The Arabic and Coptic Versions* (London: Williams and Norgate, 1904), 25–28.

6. Camplani and Contardi, "Remarks on the Textual Contribution," 148–51.

fifth or sixth century.[7] CA does not mention ordination at all, though it clearly spells out the expectations of clergy and their roles throughout the document.

What is clear, is that the process leading up to the ordination of a bishop—and the lower clergy—in CH is very similar to what is described in early non-liturgical Egyptian sources.[8] In mid-fourth-century and early fifth-century Egypt this process appeared to involve clerical choice, an acclamation of the people, and then ordination.[9] This general process is confirmed in the earliest liturgical texts, though later texts of the Coptic Rite provide much more detail,[10] and there is also evidence for the process in patristic accounts about schismatic communities and their clergy in Egypt.[11] The ordination process also entailed some form of examination and an enthronement, both of which are indicated in this canon or in CH 4: "except the sitting on the seat."[12]

Concerning the role of the presbyters in the ordination of their bishop, there was a long history in Egypt of presbyters being involved in the ordination of the patriarch

7. For a summary of the text, see Mihálykó, *The Christian Liturgical Papyri*, 24n77, 107, and 260. Sources in Nubia are totally absent; see Heinzgerd Brakmann, "Defunctus adhuc loquitur. Gottesdienst und Gebetsliteratur der untergegangenen Kirche in Nubien," *Archiv für Liturgiewissenschaft* 48 (2006): 326–28.

8. For a general overview, see Everett Ferguson, *Early Church at Work and Worship, Volume One: Ministry, Ordination, Covenant, and Canon* (Eugene, OR: Cascade Books, 2013), 86–91, 125–26, and 148–52.

9. Ferguson, *Early Church at Work and Worship, Volume One*, 62, 65, and 125–26; Wipszycka, *Alexandrian Church*, 127–31.

10. Wipszycka, *Alexandrian Church*, 132–34.

11. Wipszycka, 134–46.

12. Ferguson, *Early Church at Work and Worship, Volume One*, 64 and 86; Wipszycka, *Alexandrian Church*, 43–60 (passim).

of Alexandria, a practice that continued into the fourth century.[13] This may be the result of the close identification between bishops and presbyters in Egypt, which appears already in Origen.[14] In fact, this close identification led to conflicts in Egypt, as exhibited by Athanasius's account of a presbyter named Colluthus who was pretending to be a bishop and was ordaining other presbyters.[15] More details on the election of the patriarch appear from the fifth century onward.[16] The historical record has also preserved the names of a number of early bishops in Egypt, as well as accounts of the organization of bishops and clergy—and in some cases their correspondence—in cities like Oxyrhynchus.[17] This

13. Ferguson, *Early Church at Work and Worship, Volume One*, 86–91; Paul F. Bradshaw, *Rites of Ordination: Their History and Theology* (Collegeville, MN: Liturgical Press, 2013), 51–52; Wipszycka, *Alexandrian Church*, 43–60. Against this consensus, Stewart suggests that these are not presbyters, but rather bishops known collectively as presbyters; see Alistair Stewart, *The Original Bishops: Office and Order in the First Christian Communities* (Grand Rapids, MI: Baker Academic, 2014), 188–99. He does leave open the possibility that this occurred in the *chora*; see Stewart, 199–201.

14. Bradshaw, *Rites of Ordination*, 43. This much Stewart also shows without having to accept his claims about whether presbyters ordained bishops in Egypt; see Stewart, *The Original Bishops*, 188–201.

15. Ferguson, *Early Church at Work and Worship, Volume One*, 64.

16. Wipszycka, *Alexandrian Church*, 149–69.

17. See, for example, Klaas Anthony Worp, "A Checklist of Bishops in Byzantine Egypt (A.D. 325–c. 750)," *Zeitschrift Für Papyrologie Und Epigraphik* 100 (1994): 283–318; AnneMarie Luijendijk, *Greetings in the Lord: Early Christians and the Oxyrhynchus Papyri*, Harvard Theological Studies 60 (Cambridge: Harvard University Press, 2008); Wipszycka, *Alexandrian Church*; AnneMarie Luijendijk, "On and Beyond Duty: Christian Clergy at Oxyrhynchus (c. 250–400)," in *Beyond Priesthood: Religious Entrepreneurs and Innovators in the Roman Empire*, ed. Richard L. Gordon, Georgia Petridou, and Jörg Rüpke, Religionsgeschichtliche Versuche Und Vorarbeiten 66 (Berlin: Walter De Gruyter, 2017), 103–26.

evidence can provide some insights into the structure of the Egyptian church in this period.

What is difficult to explain is why CH does not mention the role of the patriarch of Alexandria in the ordination of a bishop. In Egypt, unlike other regions, the patriarch participated at an early date in the ordination of every Egyptian bishop, including those in the *chora*. In fact, new evidence has shed light on the growing institutionalization of the church in the *chora* in the mid- to late third century under the leadership of the bishop of Alexandria.[18] Bishop Sotas of Oxyrhynchus, for instance, was ordained by the bishop of Alexandria (Maximus) in the third century, a practice that appears to have been becoming the norm in this period.[19]

By the fourth century, Egyptian bishops were normally ordained in Alexandria as indicated by the Council of Nicaea can. 6 (325 CE). As Ewa Wipszycka notes:

> Whenever a bishop died, the local clergy, the notables, the people, and probably also the bishops of the neighbouring dioceses would decide on the choice of a candidate or, if unanimity was not forthcoming, of more than one candidate. Delegates would then set out for Alexandria in order to present the candidature(s) to the patriarch, who, however, was not bound in any way and could consecrate somebody else.[20]

A possible exception to this may have occurred in Pentapolis/ Cyrenaica (modern Libya), which was part of the Alexandrian

---

18. Ewa Wipszycka, "The Institutional Church," in *Egypt in the Byzantine World, 300–700*, ed. Roger S. Bagnall, 1. paperback ed. (Cambridge: Cambridge University Press, 2010), 331–49.

19. Luijendijk, *Greetings in the Lord*; Luijendijk, "On and Beyond Duty," 107. See also Wipszycka, "The Institutional Church."

20. Wipszycka, *Alexandrian Church*, 112–13 and 127–31.

Church, but the evidence is very vague. In a letter to the patriarch of Alexandria in the mid-fourth century, Bishop Synesius of Cyrene, metropolitan of Pentapolis, notes the ordination of a Nicene bishop by a single bishop, writing: "The election was positively unlawful, as I have learned from the older men, inasmuch as he was not consecrated either in Alexandria or by three here, even though the assent to the ordination had been given thence."[21] Wipszycka notes it is not clear if this meant that ordinations could be performed by three local bishops in Pentapolis with the patriarch's consent.[22] It is also worth noting that, unlike Egypt, Pentapolis had metropolitans, despite being under the patriarch's jurisdiction.

This raises the question: why do CH 2 and 3 (see below), and the sacramentary of Sarapion of Thmuis for that matter, contain an ordination prayer for a bishop? The inclusion of the process and prayer for the ordination of a bishop in CH may simply be a testament to its source-text (ApTrad) and the use of the same prayer for presbyters in CH 4. In other words, this could be a sign of the conservative nature of liturgical sources and the church orders in particular. But this does not explain the inclusion of an ordination prayer in the sacramentary of Sarapion of Thmuis. In analyzing the episcopal ordination prayer in that collection, it is important to note that the ecclesial landscape in fourth-century Thmuis was quite turbulent given the presence of competing bishops. As a result, "it becomes quite tempting to view Prayer 14 as a piece of episcopal propaganda intended to underscore the authority of the bishop as the genuine (γνήσιος) guardian of apos-

---

21. Wipszycka, 147. For the whole letter and another treatment, see Wipszycka, 295–98.

22. Wipszycka, 148.

tolic tradition against the continued threat of Melitianism."[23] While this does not suggest that Sarapion's prayer is a fiction, it is worth considering if it was included in the collection as a way to bolster the authority of the bishop, rather than provide directions for how to ordain a new bishop.

But it is not just CH and Sarapion that seem to preserve a local treatment of the ordination process of a bishop in a period when episcopal ordinations appear to have occurred in Alexandria. CB, which was known to have circulated in Egypt, contains an ordination ritual in canon 46 that also does not mention the patriarch.[24] Based on this, the ordination rituals described in the text are thought to reflect Syrian rather than Egyptian practice. This, of course, is a bit circular in its reasoning, but the disputed provenance of the document on other grounds makes it dubious that CB reflects native Egyptian practice, though it was likely adapted to the Egyptian context. Interestingly, CB 46 shows some parallels to the process of ordination in CH 2 and 3; however, CB also appears to be a product of a later date, since it seems to be influenced by ApCons VIII.[25]

Later Egyptian practice may help explain the inclusion of an ordination prayer in CH and the sacramentary of Sarapion of Thmuis, though of course one must be cautious when drawing parallels to later practices. Nevertheless, Heinzgerd Brakmann has observed that in the ritual for the installation of a bishop in his local church in later Coptic sources, the

---

23. Maxwell E. Johnson, *The Prayers of Sarapion of Thmuis: A Literary, Liturgical, and Theological Analysis*, Orientalia Christiana Analecta 249 (Rome: Pontifico Istituto Orientale, 1995), 156.

24. Wipszycka, *Alexandrian Church*, 275.

25. Camplani and Contardi, "Remarks on the Textual Contribution," 148–51.

ritual included a repetition of the handlaying and consecration prayer.[26] The readings for this ritual (though without a description of the ritual itself) are preserved is P.Ryl.Copt. 60 from the tenth or eleventh century, indicating that some enthronement ritual was used by that time.[27] Earlier fragments of the ritual may be preserved in P.Ryl.Copt. 23 (noted above) and in P.Lond.Copt. I 514, which is from the Fayum and dated to the ninth or tenth century.[28] P.Ryl.Copt. 23 may be an ordination prayer for a bishop or a prayer for his enthronement in his diocese, since it calls the recipient of the prayer the successor of the apostles and includes an epiclesis. Similarly, Ágnes Mihálykó in her description of P.Lond.Copt. I 514, which is "a long litany hailing Victor, the bishop of Arsinoe," notes that this text may have been used on "the enthronement of the bishop, or a feast at the return of the bishop to his see after his consecration in Alexandria. Another setting for the litany could be his visit to a monastery, which is a special feast day, witnessed in New York MLM M 575."[29] All of this may point to an earlier practice of enthronement in the Egyptian tradition.

Based on this suggestion, it is possible that the rubrics and prayer in CH 2 and 3, as well as the prayer for the ordi-

26. Heinzgerd Brakmann, "Zur Evangeliar-Auflegung bei der Ordination koptischer bischöfe," in *Eulogêma: Studies in Honor of Robert Taft, S.J.*, ed. Ephrem Carr et al. (Rome: Pontificio Ateneo S. Anselmo, 1993), 62–66, especially 63n36. For more on the early ordination rites in the Egyptian tradition, see Brakmann, "Pseudoapostolische Ordinationsgebete in apostolischen Kirchen," 86–98.

27. W. E. Crum, *Catalogue of the Coptic Manuscripts in the Collection of the John Rylands Library* (Manchester: University Press, 1909), no. 60.

28. Mihálykó, *The Christian Liturgical Papyri*, 24n77. For later evidence from Nubia, see Brakmann, "Defunctus," 327–28.

29. Mihálykó, *The Christian Liturgical Papyri*, 54n77.

nation of the bishop in Sarapion's sacramentary (Prayer 14), may have been used for the enthronement of a bishop, or even for sending the bishop to the patriarch in Alexandria. The context for both prayers in CH 2 and 3 and Sarapion's prayerbook are vague enough, though both prayers read as ordination prayers. However, if the consecration prayer, or something like it, was substantially repeated at the enthronement in later sources, this may explain why these prayers are included in CH and the sacramentary of Sarapion. It is worth noting that an enthronement is also implied in CH 4, but an enthronement is not mentioned in CH 2 or 3. It is even possible, whatever its origins, that this ritual came to be seen as an enthronement in the later Egyptian tradition.

It is also possible that the role of the Alexandrian patriarch in the ordinations of bishops in his suffrage sees was much more contested in the fourth century than the evidence has suggested. While in some places the bishop of Alexandria exerted control over the ordination of bishops already in the third century, like in the case of Bishop Sotas of Oxyrhynchus, perhaps this was not always and everywhere the case, as exhibited by the mid-fourth-century letter of Synesius. It would be seemingly inconceivable, however, even in the farthest Egyptian backwaters, for the patriarch not to be involved in some way in an episcopal ordination in Egypt much later than the mid-fourth century. It is unlikely that by the late fourth century any Egyptian center would receive CH (or any other text for that matter) and not alter it to reflect the role of the patriarch, even if the text was preserving an archaism. At the same time, it should be noted that despite being dated to a slightly later period in Egypt (sixth century), CB was not conformed to this Egyptian practice. Perhaps this speaks to a dissenting community in Egypt at this time or a historical archaism. Or, again, perhaps the hold of the bishop of Alexandria over the ordination process in all of Egypt and its suffrage sees was not as strong as suggested by the literary records and took longer to be formalized. In any event, CH either points to a historical archaism, some sort of political/ ecclesial propaganda, a rapidly declining practice preserved in some far-off places, or some combination of the three. What is known about Egyptian ordination in this period does not preclude an Egyptian provenance, and texts like Prayer 14 in the sacramentary of Sarapion and the account of ordination in CB already complexify the traditional narrative. Given that even Stewart is forced to see CH as a final product of Egypt, all of this likely points to an early date for CH's arrival in Egypt, perhaps in an Egyptian center like Pentapolis that had not yet fully conformed to the emerging norms of the Alexandrian church, rather than the later dating proposed by Stewart. It also must have in some way mirrored or fit with Egyptian practice somewhere, since it would otherwise have been conformed to local practice.

CH §3

Prayer over him who becomes Bishop, and Order of the Liturgy

[3a]

'O God, Father of our Lord Jesus Christ, Father of mercies and God of all comfort, dwelling on high and looking upon the lowly, knowing all things before they come to pass, you who have fixed the boundaries of the Church, who have decreed from Adam that there should exist a righteous race—by the intermediary of this bishop—that is [the race] of great Abraham, you who have established authorities and powers, look upon N. [your servant] with your power and mighty Spirit, which you have given to the holy apostles by our Lord Jesus Christ, your only Son. They are those who have founded the Church in every place, for the honor and glory of your holy name.

Since you know the heart of everyone, make him shepherd your people blamelessly, so that he may be worthy of tending your great and holy flock, make his life higher than [that] of all his people, without dispute; make him envied by everyone by reason of his virtue; accept his prayers and his offerings which he will offer you day and night; and let them be for you a sweet-smelling savor. Give him, Lord, the episcopate, a merciful spirit, and the authority to forgive sins; give him power to loosen every bond of the oppression of demons, to cure the sick and crush Satan under his feet swiftly; through our Lord Jesus Christ, through *whom be glory to you, with him and the Holy Spirit, to the ages of ages. Amen.'*

And all the people say, 'Amen.'

[3b]

After that they are all to turn towards him and give him the kiss of peace, because he is worthy of it.

Then the deacon brings the offerings, and he who has become bishop lays his hand on the offerings with the presbyters, saying, 'The Lord be with all.'

The people reply, 'And with your spirit'

He says, 'Lift up your hearts.'

They reply, 'We have [them] to the Lord.'

He says, 'Let us give thanks to the Lord.'

They reply, 'It is fitting and right,' that is to say, 'it is fitting.'

After that, he says the prayer and completes the liturgy.

[3c]

If there is any oil, he prays over it in this way, though not the same expressions, but the same meaning. If there are any first fruits, anything edible, which someone has brought, he prays over it, and in his prayer, blesses the fruit which is brought to him.

In each prayer which is said over each item, there is said at the end of the prayer, 'Glory to you, Father, Son, and Holy Spirit, to the ages of ages. Amen.'

The first part of this canon (§3a-b) is largely taken from ApTrad 3 and 4. It is worth noting that the prayer for the ordination of the bishop in this canon is, as Bradshaw notes, "the only prayer from [ApTrad] which has been substantially adopted in this work."[1] At the same time, Bradshaw has also observed that the episcopal prayer was stripped of its "high priestly language" and as a result "it is tempting to wonder if once again it has retained a more primitive text, but a close comparison of the two suggests that this is unlikely, and that it is the compiler of the *Canons of Hippolytus* who has been responsible for deleting an aspect of the episcopal office that was foreign to his local tradition."[2] Of course, it still cannot be discounted that CH might be providing an earlier reading of the text, especially since this seems to be the case elsewhere in the document and given Bradshaw's proposed original form of the prayer.[3] If this prayer was stripped of its high priestly language when it was taken over into CH from ApTrad, this could be the result of a close connection between bishops and presbyters.

Both Bradshaw and Stewart have noted some parallels to the intercession of the patriarch in the Egyptian prayers of the faithful and in the Egyptian anaphora of St. Mark (henceforth MARK).[4] They have also noted that the first stanza

1. Bradshaw, *The Canons of Hippolytus*, 12.

2. Bradshaw, *Rites of Ordination*, 68.

3. Paul F. Bradshaw, "The Ordination Prayers in the So-Called *Apostolic Tradition*," *Vigiliae Christianae* 75 (2021): 125.

4. Bradshaw, *The Canons of Hippolytus*, 12; Stewart, *The Canons of Hippolytus*, 77n27. Some of these echoes are already in the prayer for the patriarch (*papas*) in the Euchologion of the Aksumite Collection (Σ51^{ra-rb}), henceforth Euch-AC, and in the oldest fully extant version of MARK preserved in the Aksumite Collection; see Emmanuel Fritsch, "Two Ancient Ge'ez Witnesses of the Anaphora of Saint Mark," in *Explorations in Eastern*

of the pre-anaphoral dialogue—"The Lord be with all"—is similar to that of MARK.[5] The omission in this canon of the anaphora that appears in the corresponding chapter of ApTrad (ApTrad 4) is significant, since the Egyptian versions of the ApTrad, including Ethiopic I, omit the eucharistic prayer, which is otherwise only preserved in the Latin and Ethiopic II[6] versions of the text. It is omitted in Ethiopic I, it appears, because other eucharistic prayers were included in the Euchologion preserved in the Aksumite Collection (Euch-AC), including an anaphora adapted from ApTrad 4.[7] Like the rest of the Aksumite Collection, Euch-AC is dated to the second half of the fifth century or first half of the sixth century and is Alexandrian.[8] The eucharistic prayer was

---

Christian Liturgy: Selected Papers of the Sixth International Congress of the Society of Oriental Liturgy, Etchmiadzin, Armenia, 11–16 September 2016, ed. Nina Glibetic and Gabriel Radle, Studies in Eastern Christian Liturgies 4 (Münster: Aschendorff Verlag, 2022), 307–8. For an edition of the text, see Valerio Polidori, *Alexandria Unveiled: An Exploration of the Most Ancient Recension of St. Mark's Liturgy.* Studi sul Cristianesimo Primitivo 4 (Coppell: Kindle Direct Publishing, 2023), 112–18. We thank Alessandro Bausi for making available to us his draft edition and translation of the Euchologion and allowing us to speak about its contents before its publication.

5. Bradshaw, *The Canons of Hippolytus*, 13; Stewart, *The Canons of Hippolytus*, 77n28. The version of MARK preserved in the Aksumite Collection also contains this feature; see Fritsch, "Two Ancient," 301.

6. This is the later Ethiopic version of ApTrad preserved in the *Sinodos*; see *Herm.Com.* 2002.

7. Emmanuel Fritsch, "How the Antiochene Anaphora of the Apostolic Tradition Became the Ge'ez Anaphora of the Apostles," in *Holy Spirit University of Kaslik, Faculty of Religious and Oriental Sciences, Institute of Liturgy and Department of Syriac and Antiochian Sciences, International Conference "Anaphora in Syriac Rites" 26–28 April 2017* (Beirut: USEK, 2017), 115–58; Fritsch, "Two Ancient."

8. See p. xvii, n. 30.

original to the text of ApTrad, since it appears in the Latin, Ethiopic II, and in another of ApTrad's derivatives, mainly TD I.23, where it has undergone some changes. As a result, the omission of the prayer from CH in the Egyptian sources points to an Egyptian context.

It is worth nothing that the phrase "give him power to loosen every bond of the oppression of demons, to cure the sick and crush Satan under his feet swiftly" seems to place the bishop (and presbyters who use the same prayer; see CH 4) as exorcists in the community. There was no order of exorcists in Egypt.[9] Earlier Origen had even indicated that any baptized Christian could perform an exorcism (*Contra Celsum* 7.4).[10] But the prayer in this canon may indicate a movement toward the clerical control of the exorcistic rites.

The end of this canon (§3c) appears to treat all at once material contained in ApTrad 5, 6, and 31-32.

9. Ewa Wipszycka, "Les ordres mineurs dans l'Église d'Egypte du IVe au VIIIe siècle," *The Journal of Juristic Papyrology* 23 (1993): 189–90.

10. Michael Fiedrowicz and Claudia Barthold, eds., *Origenes, Contra Celsum – Gegen Celsus*, Fontes Christiani 50.5 (Freiburg: Herder, 2011), 1186.

CH §4

Concerning the Ordination
of Presbyters

When a presbyter is ordained, one is to do for him everything which one does for the bishop, except the sitting on the seat. One is to pray over him the whole prayer of the bishop, except only the name of the bishop. The presbyter is equal to the bishop in everything except the seat and ordination, because he has not been given the power to ordain.

Here CH differs from ApTrad 7 in having only the bishop lay hands on the presbyter, and the prayer from ApTrad 7 is omitted. Stewart suggests that there is an "equation of presbyter and bishop" in this canon and that "rather than reflecting a primitive presbyteral order, however, this represents a situation in which the original Asian presbyteral patrons have developed into an ascetic group, led by a bishop."[1] There is nothing to suggest the development of an ascetic group; however, there are possible reasons to see an equation of presbyter and bishop. In fact, this could easily point to an Egyptian context. In looking at CA, Wipszycka notes that CA is very clear in equating bishops and presbyters:

1. Stewart, *The Canons of Hippolytus*, 46.

From Canon 10 we learn that in the eyes of God presbyters are equal to bishops as they are responsible for their 'region' in the same way as the bishops are responsible for the city and the regions under their auspices. This is a very important declaration, meaning that we are dealing with such a stage of development of Egyptian Christian communities in which a network of autonomous non-episcopal churches called *katholikai* existed, which were run by the presbyters.[2]

This system of "*katholikai* flourished as early as the second quarter of the fourth century."[3] But of course, these remain distinct offices, and so the bishop and presbyter were not quite the same. As a result, there is a tension in the text.

The "omission" of the presbyteral prayer here in CH may be the result of the local equation of presbyter and bishop, but it is also very possible that this prayer had not yet made its way into ApTrad at the time of the CH's composition. As noted above, the prayer in ApTrad 7.2-5 is in the Latin and Ethiopic II and is also paralleled in ApCons and TD, but it is not in Ethiopic I or here in CH.[4]

The equation of presbyter and bishop at the start of CH 4 is a holdover from ApTrad 7, though CH 4 makes it clear they are not equal despite using the same form. This fits comfortably with the Egyptian context of the fourth century, as noted above with CH 2, and likely explains the form for the ordination of the presbyter in CH 3. About this equation and how it may have shaped CH 4, Everett Ferguson writes:

2. Wipszycka, "A Certain Bishop," 96.

3. Wipszycka, 96n11.

4. The *Herm. Com.* 2002 sees this prayer, while having ancient features and parallels exclusively to the prayer in the sacramentary of Sarapion of Thmuis, "as a subsequent addition to the core document, even though the prayer itself may be very old." *Herm. Com.* 2002, 59.

The bishop differs from a presbyter only in the special seat given him and in the power of ordination. The similarity was enforced by directing that a similar Prayer bc stated except for the name "bishop." The directions of the *Apostolic Tradition* apparently were misunderstood and its Prayer for a presbyter was simply omitted. The obvious reason for the compiler taking this alternative and giving the directions which he did was that he had a theory of the ministry based on the recollection of an earlier state of affairs, when there was no great difference between presbyters and bishops and when ordination was restricted to the chief minister (who occupied the chair) for the sake of the order of the church.[5]

Again, it is also possible the prayer is omitted because CH here provides an earlier witness to ApTrad along the lines given by Ferguson. In any event, like with the ordination of a bishop, there is abundant evidence for an extended examination of presbyters in Egypt as is implied in CH, along with the duties they are expected to fulfill.[6] CA, for instance, provides an abundance of regulations and expectations for presbyters. In fact, as Wipszycka notes, "The author writes with special emphasis about presbyters. The Canons [CA] open with a very significant text: 'These are the laws of the presbyters.'"[7]

The absence of an ordination prayer for the presbyters in CH may have parallels in the sacramentary of Sarapion, where Johnson has persuasively argued that the ordination prayer for deacons (Prayer 12) and the prayer for bishops (Prayer 14) are theologically and literarily distinct from the prayer for the ordination of presbyters (Prayer 13). He has also argued

---

5. Ferguson, *Early Church at Work and Worship, Volume One*, 89.
6. Wipszycka, *Alexandrian Church*, 308–25.
7. Wipszycka, "A Certain Bishop," 96.

that Prayer 12 and Prayer 14 are likely later than Prayer 13.[8] Perhaps presbyters and bishops were originally ordained in Thmuis, like in CH, using the same prayer, in this case Prayer 13. There is nothing in Prayer 13 that could not apply to both presbyters and bishops, and given that Prayer 13 appears to be an earlier text than Prayers 12 and 14, it could suggest that this was originally the prayer for the bishop too. In fact, Johnson notes that "Prayer 13 may well represent a rather early prayer for the presbyterate, a prayer which corresponds to the pre-Nicene presbyteral-episcopal style of church leadership within the Egyptian tradition."[9] This may also explain why Prayer 12 and Prayer 14 are closely related, because they were added when distinctions were emerging between the presbyterate and episcopacy in particular. What we may see in comparing Sarapion to CH is that both originally used the same ordination prayer for bishops and presbyters.

The lack of a prayer in CH for presbyters tracks with the Egyptian evidence that strongly equated presbyters and bishops, though this was an older Egyptian practice that was already giving way in the mid-fourth century. The note not to sit in the seat is likely the result of thrones being placed even in non-episcopal churches, something seen in the archaeological evidence from Egypt, albeit mostly from a later date.[10] But it is also likely an indication that there was an enthronement as part of the episcopal ordination, something that seems confirmed by other Egyptian texts as well (see the discussion in CH 2 above).

8. Johnson, *The Prayers of Sarapion*, 92–95 and 148–62.

9. Johnson, 153.

10. Peter Grossmann, *Christliche Architektur in Ägypten* (Leiden: Brill, 2002), especially 189–91.

CH §5

Concerning the Ordination of Deacons

When a deacon is ordained, one is to do for him according to the same rules, and one is to say this prayer over him.

He is not appointed for the presbyterate, but for the diaconate, as a servant of God. He serves the bishop and the presbyters in everything, not only at the time of the liturgy, and he serves also the sick of the people, those who have nobody, and he informs the bishop so that he may pray over them or give to them what they need. He also serves those people whose poverty is not apparent but who are in need. They are to serve also those who have the alms of the bishops, and they are able to give to widows, to orphans, and to the poor. He is to perform all the services. So this in truth is the deacon of whom Christ has said, 'He who serves me, my Father will honor him.' The bishop lays his hand on the deacon and prays over him, saying:

'O God, Father of our Lord Jesus Christ, we beseech you, pour out your Holy Spirit on N. [your servant]; count him among those who serve you according to all your will like Stephen and his companions; fill him with power and wisdom like Stephen; make him triumph over all the powers of the Devil by the sign of your cross with which you sign him; make his life without sin before all men and an example for many, so that he may save a multitude in the holy Church without shame; and accept all his service; through our Lord Jesus Christ, through whom be glory to you, with him and the Holy Spirit, to the ages of ages. Amen.'

This canon is a thorough reworking of ApTrad 8; however, CH interweaves multiple texts of ApTrad (8, 29B, and 34). At the same time, it follows TD I.33-34 and 38 more closely here than ApTrad, pointing to the complex relationship between CH and TD. The prayer in CH is not the same as that given in ApTrad 8, and has correspondences with ApCons VIII.18 as well as Sarapion's Prayer 12, though Stewart does not reference Sarapion.[1] This may, again, suggest that this prayer in ApTrad was not originally part of the text, since it also does not appear in Ethiopic I. The ordination of a deacon in the later Coptic Rite also includes a prayer with many parallels.[2] Stewart argues that a consignation was possibly part of the rite,[3] which may or may not be the case, and as a result suggests that this points to an Antiochene context.[4] This seems a tenuous connection, and we know of a consignation, albeit in episcopal ordination, in Egypt[5] and in the Coptic ordination rite for the deaconate.[6] Like with the ordination of bishops and presbyters, there is abundant evidence—here again CA can be referenced—for an extended examination of deacons in Egypt as is implied in CH, along with the duties they are expected to fulfill.[7]

1. Bradshaw, *The Canons of Hippolytus*, 14; Stewart, *The Canons of Hippolytus*, 42 and 47.

2. Paul F. Bradshaw, *Ordination Rites of the Ancient Churches of East and West* (New York: Pueblo, 1990), 143–44.

3. Bradshaw, *The Canons of Hippolytus*, 14.

4. Stewart, *The Canons of Hippolytus*, 47.

5. Wipszycka, *Alexandrian Church*, 133.

6. Bradshaw, *Ordination Rites of the Ancient Churches of East and West*, 144.

7. Wipszycka, *Alexandrian Church*, 308–25.

CH §7

Concerning the Choice of Reader
and of Subdeacon

When one chooses a reader, he is to have the virtues of the deacon. The hand is not laid on him, but the bishop is to give him the Gospel.

The subdeacon [is to be appointed] according to this arrangement: he is not to be ordained while still celibate and unmarried, unless his neighbors bear witness for him and testify that he has kept himself away from women during the time of his maturity.

The hand is not laid on someone in the state of celibacy, unless he has reached his maturity or is entering into mature age and is thought [worthy], when one bears witness for him.

The subdeacon and the reader, when they pray alone, are to keep themselves behind, and the subdeacon is to serve behind the deacon.

CH merges ApTrad 11, 12, and 13. In its incorporation of the making of female virgins in ApTrad 12, CH 7 applies this to both men and women, as does TD I.46. However, TD makes it clear, following ApTrad 12, that a laying on of hands is not used to set aside those who wish to be virgins, while the text of CH is more ambiguous and seems to suggest that a laying on of hands can be offered for ascetics (i.e., for virginity alone) after maturity has been reached. This text in CH has often been treated as a reference to ordination, likely to the subdeaconate, given the switch to "he" in the canon.[1] Interestingly, however, in the slightly later euchologion from the Aksumite Collection (Euch-AC) there is a prayer for the laying on of hands on virgins (explicitly stated as male and female in the text) and nuns.[2] This seems to be closely related to the practice described here in CH, and represents a different practice than that outlined in TD.

1. Bradshaw, *The Canons of Hippolytus*, 15.

2. Euch-AC, Σ57[va]. There may also be some connection here to P.Bal. I 30 though the content of that material is difficult to judge; see Ágnes T. Mihálykó, "Writing the Christian Liturgy in Egypt (3rd to 9th Century)" (PhD Diss., University of Oslo, 2016), 267–78.

CH §9b

[Concerning . . . the Function
of Widows]

*Established widows should not be ordained—there are in effect
for them the precepts of the Apostle. They are not to be ordained,
but one is to pray over them, because ordination is for men.
The function of widows is important by reason of all that is
incumbent upon them: frequent prayer, the ministry of the sick,
and frequent fasting.*

The treatment of widows here is a simplification of Ap-
Trad 10, though their ministry in CH now also includes a
specific ministry to the sick. Both Bradshaw and Stewart note
parallels here to ACO 21 and *Didascalia* 15.[1] This seems
to suggest an Asian origin to Stewart, though this is hardly
enough to indicate this, especially given the important role
of widows in Egypt.[2] The distinction that widows are not
to be ordained is consistent with the way documents like CA

1. Bradshaw, *The Canons of Hippolytus*, 16; Stewart, *The Canons of Hippolytus*, 41–42 and 89.
2. Wipszycka, *Alexandrian Church*, 115, 173–81, 357–59.

talk about the clergy (bishops, stewards, priests, and deacons) being charged with their care.[3]

3. Canon 16 (Arabic), Riedel and Crum, *The Canons of Athanasius of Alexandria: The Arabic and Coptic Versions*, 26–28; Canon 61 (Arabic and Coptic), Ibid., pp. 40–41 and 126–29; Canon 70 (Arabic and Coptic), Ibid., pp. 44–47 and 133–35; and Canon 84 (Arabic), Ibid., p. 51.

CH §12

Prohibition of Several Occupations: He who is involved in them is only to be received after Repentance

Whoever becomes director of a theatre, or a wrestler, or a runner, or teaches music, or plays before the processions, or teaches the art of the gladiator, or is a hunter, or a hairdresser, or fights with savage beasts, or is a priest of idols, all these, one is not to reveal to them any of the holy word, until they are purified first from these impure occupations. Then, during forty days they are to hear the word, and if they are worthy, they are to be baptized. The teacher of the Church is the one who judges this matter.

A schoolmaster who teaches little children, if he has not a livelihood by which to live except for that, may educate, if he reveals at all times to those he teaches and confesses that what the Gentiles call gods are demons, and says before them every day there is no divinity except the Father, the Son, and the Holy Spirit. If he can teach his pupils the excellent word of the poet, and better still if he can teach them the faith of the word of truth, for that he shall have a reward.

The whole canon has been modified from ApTrad 16 and 17. The reference to a forty-day exclusive catechumenate replaces that of a three-year period, which appears in all versions of ApTrad. While there may be nothing explicitly Egyptian in this, there is also nothing explicitly Cappadocian. At the same time, Nicholas Russo has shown that Egyptian sources reveal forty-day, quadragesimal fasting regimens as a hallmark of the early Alexandrian tradition.[1] The ubiquity of that pattern, in fact, and its use for varied circumstances (e.g., post-baptismal penance, catechesis, pre-baptismal purgation for those holding certain occupations, etc.) further suggests that it was likely to have been long established. Similarly, Charles Renoux has shown that at the beginning of the year a forty-day fast did, in fact, take place in Egypt,[2] though he claimed erroneously that it did not refer to Jesus' own forty-day fast in the wilderness, which is contradicted by Peter I of Alexandria's reference to a forty-day period of penance in his canonical letter (306 CE).[3]

To assert that this forty-day catechetical period in CH 12 is Lent would also mean assuming that the catechumenate took place in preparation for Paschal Baptism, which is not assumed anywhere in CH nor in the various versions of ApTrad. In fact, where Pascha is discussed, for example, in CH 22, there is no reference whatsoever to baptism. There is no reference to a baptismal day or season in CH 12 and the forty-day catechumenate could apply equally to Epiphany, Paschal, or other baptismal days. See further on this below in our comments on CH 20.

There is also a significant modification in the second part of the canon on the schoolmaster. This material has tan-

---

1. Nicholas Russo, *The Origins of Lent* (Ph.D. Diss., University of Notre Dame,.2009), 389ff.

2. For the text of Peter I of Alexandria's canonical letter here, see ANF 6, 278.

3. Charles (Athanase) Renoux, "L'Annonciation du rite arménien et l'Épiphanie," *OCP* 71 (2005): 336–42.

talizing connections to an Egyptian philosophical school context, which emerges in the fifth century but which likely had fourth-century roots.[4] Of course similar confraternities emerged in Syria in the fourth century and these confraternities may even be tied to the Egyptian collection of texts known as the Bodmer Library.[5] The reference that he "says before them every day there is no [God] except the Father, the Son, and the Holy Spirit" parallels the "One God—Jesus the Lord" acclamation common in the ancient Christian world, but especially attested from a school setting in the "Barcelona Papyrus"[6] and in the treatise "On the One Judge."[7] The reference to the "words of the poets (ποιητής)" and "the word of truth" may bear some similarity to the classical literature and acrostic in the Barcelona Papyrus[8] and other ancient Christian Egyptian libraries like the Bodmer Library,[9] which were connected to philosophical schools and ascetical communities. There are also parallels here to the Ethiopian Mystagogical

4. Ewa Wipszycka, "Les confreries dans la vie religieuse de l'Egypte chretienne," in *Proceedings of the Twelfth International Congress of Papyrology*, American Studies in Papyrology 7 (Toronto: A.M. Hakkert Ltd., 1970), 511–25; Edward Jay Watts, *City and School in Late Antique Athens and Alexandria*, The Transformation of the Classical Heritage 41 (Berkeley: University of California Press, 2006), especially Ch. 8: Alexandrian Schools of the Fifth Century.

5. Arthur Vööbus, *History of Asceticism in the Syrian Orient*, vol. 2, CSCO 184 (Louvain: Secrétariat du CorpusSCO, 1958), I: pp. 97–103; II: 331–42; Cristiano Berolli, "Tracce di ascetismo in ὁ δεσπό[τ]ης πρὸς τοὺς πά[σχο]ντας," *Adamantius* 21 (2015): 136–43.

6. Chase, *The Anaphoral Tradition*, Ch. 5.

7. Bausi, "The Treatise *On the One Judge* (CAe 6260) in the *Aksumite Collection* (CAe1047)."

8. Chase, *The Anaphoral Tradition*, Ch. 3.

9. Chase, Ch. 3.

Catechesis (Ethio-MC), copied from a Greek exemplar in Alexandria in the fifth century.[10]

10. Emmanuel Fritsch, "The *Order of the Mystery:* An Ancient Catechesis Preserved in BnF Ethiopic Ms d'Abbadie 66-66bis (Fifteenth Century) with a Liturgical Commentary," in *Studies in Oriental Liturgy: Proceedings of the Fifth International Congress of the Society of Oriental Liturgy, New York, 10–15 June 2014*, ed. Bert Groen et al. (Leuven: Peeters, 2019), 195–263; Mihálykó, *The Christian Liturgical Papyri*, 44–45.

CH §16

Concerning the Christian who has a Concubine and is Married to Another

A Christian who has a concubine yet marries another, especially
if the concubine has had a child by him, is considered a homicide
unless he catches her in fornication.

This canon is based on ApTrad 16.15-17, and Stewart notes that a similar context is described in GCN 7.1:[1] "A man who fornicates, whilst having a wife, is worthless, and an infanticide."[2] Stewart argues that this points away from a Western context for CH, at least, since concubinage and men leaving their concubines were common in the West.[3] The similarities here to GCN are striking and point to an Egyptian context.

1. Stewart, *The Canons of Hippolytus*, 101n65.

2. Stewart, *The Gnomai*, 55.

3. Stewart, *The Canons of Hippolytus*, 101n65. Here he finds support in Philip Lyndon Reynolds, *Marriage in the Western Church: The Christianization of Marriage during the Patristic and Early Medieval Periods* (Boston: Brill, 2001), 162–67.

CH §17

[17a] Concerning the Free Woman: What she [must] do

A free woman is not to wear jewelry in church, even if it is a custom sanctioned by her husband. She is not to leave her hair loose, that is in plaits, in the house of God. She is not to wear braids on the head when she wishes to partake of the holy mysteries. She is not to give her children, those whom she has borne, to nurses, but she is to raise them herself according to the law of marriage. She is not to neglect her housework. She is not to answer her husband back in anything, even if she knows more than he, but she is to remember God at all times. [If] she knows more than men, she is not to reveal [it] to anyone, but she is to serve her husband like a master. She is to concern herself with the poor, her neighbors; she is to concern herself with the first offerings in place of a vain adorning, because you will not find a woman adorned with precious stones as beautiful as one like this, who is beautiful in her nature and excellence alone. Let this make them careful to be pure and not love pleasure; they are not to be inclined to laugh and are not to talk at all in church, because the house of God is not a place for talk but a place of prayer and reverence. Anyone who talks in church is to be expelled and is not to partake that time of the mysteries.

[17b]

A catechumen who is worthy of the light should not be prevented by time, because his conduct is a proof: the teacher of the Church is the one who judges this matter.

All of this canon, except the final sentence (§17b), which is paralleled in ApTrad 17.2, is a new creation.[1] There are some parallels in the discussion of women's jewelry to ApTrad 21.5.[2] The new material has some parallels to GCN 3.2, 4.3, and 4.5.[3] Stewart notes issues with the phrase "even if it is a custom sanctioned by her husband," which can also be read as "not even in the year of her marriage." The latter, Stewart suggests, could be a reference to the Roman wedding veil (*flammeum*) or a reference to wearing jewelry from a woman's dowry.[4] There are also some parallels here to CA canon 44 (Arabic and Coptic), though in that text the prohibition against women wearing jewelry at church is directed at the wives of priests: "No priest shall suffer his wife to adorn herself with gold or silver or precious stones or with antimony or anklets or head-dresses or costly stuffs; for this guise is not for the children of the church. . . . For the priest's wife eateth of the bread of the altar; for this cause she must needs walk

1. Bradshaw, *The Canons of Hippolytus*, 19.
2. Charles Cosgrove, "A Woman's Unbound Hair in the Greco-Roman World, with Special Reference to the Story of the 'Sinful Woman' in Luke 7:36-50," *Journal of Biblical Literature* 124 (2005): 685–86.
3. Stewart, *The Canons of Hippolytus*, 17, 30, and 103–5.
4. Stewart, 103n67.

seemly."[5] A similar concern about jewelry appears in SD VIII.4.[6] The parallels to GCN, CA, and SD may point to an Egyptian context, but there is nothing that readily points to a specific geographical location.

5. Riedel and Crum, *The Canons of Athanasius of Alexandria: The Arabic and Coptic Versions*, 34–35.
6. Hyvernat, "Le Syntagma Doctrinae," 127–28.

CH §18

Concerning the Midwives and the Separation of Women from Men during Prayer: The Girls are to Veil Their Head; Concerning the Women who give Birth

After the teacher has finished instructing each day, they are to pray separated from the Christians.

The midwives are not to partake of the mysteries until they have been purified. Their purification shall be thus: if the child which they have delivered is male, twenty days; if it is female, forty days. They are not to the neglect the confinements, but they are to pray to God for her who is confined. If she goes to the house of God before being purified, she is to pray with the catechumens who have not yet been received and have not been [judged] worthy to be accepted.

The women are to be separated in a place. They are not to give the kiss to any man.

The teacher is to lay the hand on the catechumens before dismissing them. The girls, when the degree of their youth is accomplished, are to cover the head, like the adult women, with their shawl, not with a thin cloth.

The woman who has given birth remains outside the holy place for forty days if the child which she has borne is male, and if it is female, eighty days. If she enters the church, she is to pray with the catechumens.

> *The midwives are to be numerous, so that they may not be outside all their life.*

This canon is largely an expansion of ApTrad 18–19.1. What has been added is the material on midwives and the material on women who have given birth. Bradshaw notes that the material that has been added in—namely, on those who give birth and when they can be allowed back into church—has parallels in the later Coptic tradition.[1] While noting Egyptian parallels, Stewart also suggests that this attests to a Judaizing tendency and has parallels in Asian or Cappadocian contexts, mainly in TD I.23, *Didascalia*, and John Chrysostom.[2] But this material is so common it cannot point to a particular context. CH also splits ApTrad 19 into two different canons, with ApTrad 19.1 being included here and ApTrad 19.2 being included at the start of CH 19a.

1. Bradshaw, *The Canons of Hippolytus*, 20.
2. Stewart, *The Canons of Hippolytus*, 22 and 42–43.

CH §19

[19a] Concerning the Catechumen who is Killed because of Witness before Baptism: He is to be Buried with the Martyrs. Concerning the Catechumens: The Conditions which the Catechumens are to fulfil during the Baptism and the Exorcism, the Order of the Liturgy of Baptism, and the Consecration of the Liturgy of the Body and the Blood

When a catechumen is arrested because of witness and killed before having been baptized, he is to be buried with all the martyrs, because he has been baptized in his own blood.

[19b] Chapter of the Catechumens

The catechumen, when he is baptized, and he who presents him, attest that he has been zealous for the commandments during the time of his catechumenate, that he has visited the sick or given to the needy, that he has kept himself from every wicked and

disgraceful word, that he has hated vainglory, despised pride, and chosen for himself humility. He confesses to the bishop that he [takes] responsibility for himself, so that the bishop is satisfied about him and considers him [worthy] of the mysteries, and that he has become truly pure, then [this bishop] reads over him the Gospel at that time, and asks him several times, 'Are you in two minds, or under pressure from anything, or driven by convention? For nobody mocks the kingdom of heaven, but it is given to those who love it with all their heart.'

Those who are to be baptized are to bathe in water on the fifth day of the week and eat. They are to fast on Friday. If there is a woman and she has her menstrual period, she is not to be baptized on that occasion but she is to wait until she is purified.

[19c]

On Saturday the bishop assembles those who are to be baptized. He makes them bow their heads towards the east, extends his hand over them, and prays and expels every evil spirit from them by his exorcism, and these never return to them from that time on through their deeds. When he has finished exorcizing them, he breathes on their face and signs their breast, their forehead, their ears, and their nose.

They are to spend all their night in the sacred word and prayers. At cockcrow, they are positioned by the water, water from a river, running and pure, prepared and sanctified.

Those who reply for the little children are to strip them of their clothes first; then those who are capable of answering for themselves; then the women are to be the last of all to divest themselves of their clothes. They are to remove their jewels, whether they are gold or otherwise, and loosen the hair of their head, for fear that something of the alien spirits should go down with them into the water of the second birth.

The bishop blesses the oil of exorcism and gives it to a presbyter; then he blesses the oil of anointing, that is the oil of thanksgiving, and gives it to another presbyter. He who holds the oil of exorcism stands on the left of the bishop and he who holds the oil of anointing stands on the right of the bishop.

He who is to be baptized turns his face towards the west and says, 'I renounce you, Satan, and all your service.' When he has said that, the presbyter anoints him with the oil of exorcism which has been blessed, so that every evil spirit may depart from him. He is handed over by a deacon to the presbyter who stands near the water. A presbyter holds his right hand and makes him turn his face towards the east, near the water. Before going down into the water, his face towards the east and standing near the water, he says this after having received the oil of exorcism: 'I believe, and I submit myself to you and to all your service, O Father, Son, and Holy Spirit.'

Thus he descends into the waters. The presbyter places his hand on his head and questions him, saying, 'Do you believe in God the Father Almighty?' He who is baptized replies, 'I believe.' Then he immerses him in the water once, his hand on his head. He questions him a second time, saying, 'Do you believe in Jesus Christ, Son of God, whom the virgin Mary bore by the Holy Spirit, who came for the salvation of the human race, who was crucified in the time of Pontius Pilate, who died and was raised from the dead on the third day, ascended into heaven, is seated at the right hand of the Father, and will come to judge the living and the dead?' He replies, 'I believe.' Then he immerses him in the water a second time. He questions him a third time, saying, 'Do you believe in the Holy Spirit, the Paraclete, flowing from the Father and the Son?' When he replies, 'I believe,' he immerses him a third time in the water. And he says each time, 'I baptize you in the name of the Father, of the Son, and of the Holy Spirit, equal Trinity.'

Then he comes up from the water. The presbyter takes the oil of thanksgiving and signs his forehead, his mouth, and his breast, and anoints all his body, his head, and his face, saying,

'I anoint you in the name of the Father, of the Son, and of the Holy Spirit.' And he wipes him with a cloth, which he keeps for him. He dresses him in his clothes, and takes him into the church.

The bishop lays his hand on all the baptized and prays thus:

'We bless you, Lord God almighty, that you have made these worthy to be born again, and have poured your Holy Spirit on them,[1] so that they become one in the body of the Church, not being excluded by alien works. Just as you have granted them forgiveness for their sins, grant them also the pledge of your kingdom; through our Lord Jesus Christ, through whom be glory to you, with him and the Holy Spirit, to ages of ages. Amen.'

Next, he signs their forehead with the oil of anointing and gives them the kiss, saying, 'The Lord be with you.' And those who have been baptized also say, 'And with your spirit.' He does this to each of the baptized. After that, they pray with all the people of the faithful and they give them the kiss and rejoice with them with cries of gladness.

Then the deacon begins the liturgy and the bishop completes the Eucharist of the body and blood of the Lord. When he has finished, he gives communion to the people, he himself standing near the table of the body and blood of the Lord. The presbyters hold the cups of the blood of Christ and other cups of milk and honey, so that those who partake may know that they are born again like little children, because little children partake of milk and honey. If there are no presbyters to hold them, the deacons are to hold them. And so the bishop gives them the body of Christ, saying, 'This is the body of Christ.' They reply, 'Amen.' He who gives them the cup says, 'This is the blood of Christ.' They reply, 'Amen.' Then they partake of the milk and honey, in remembrance of the age to come, and of the sweetness of its blessings, which does not return to bitterness and does not fade away.

---

1. This prayer appears to be closer to the Latin translation of ApTrad than to Ethiopic I, in that the Holy Spirit is treated as a gift already received in Baptism (i.e., the Holy Spirit has been "poured" upon the newly baptized). Hence, the petition is not for the Holy Spirit but for the "pledge of your kingdom."

[19d]

Thus they become complete Christians and are fed with the body of Christ. They will strive in wisdom, so that their life may shine with virtue, not before each other [only], but also before the Gentiles, so that they may imitate them and become Christians and see that the progress of those who have been illuminated is high and better than the common behavior of people.

[19e]

As for those who have been baptized and those also who have fasted with them, they are not to taste anything before partaking of the body of Christ, because that will not be counted to them as a fast but as a sin. He who tastes anything before partaking of the body disobeys and despises God. But when the liturgy is finished, he can eat what he wishes.

[19f]

All the catechumens are to assemble one with another, and a single teacher is to be sufficient for them, who will instruct them sufficiently. They are to pray and bend the knee. They are not to taste anything before those who have been baptized have received the body and the blood.

Stewart has argued for an Asian/Syrian origin for the rites of initiation in CH primarily based on the presence of an *apotaxis* and a *syntaxis*, the form of the baptismal creed, and the post-baptismal rites.[2] However, there is nothing particularly Cappadocian/Syrian about the initiation materials in CH. CH witnesses, in fact, to what appears to be the traditional Egyptian location of the blessings of oil and water at the beginning of the baptismal rite, which was later moved to the locations for the pre-baptismal and post-baptismal anointings within the rite as seen in the Baptismal Ritual in the Aksumite Collection (henceforth BR-AC)[3] and the Euch-AC, before eventually being split off from the initiatory rites entirely around the ninth or tenth century.[4] The forty days of preparation (noted below in CH 20), pre-judged by Stewart in his translation and introduction to be "Lent," have no parallels in any of the documents derived from ApTrad, where, as noted above in CH 12, a forty-day catechumenate replaces a three-year period from ApTrad 16. While this may reflect an established pre-paschal "Lent," as Stewart translates and assumes, we noted above that it appears to be consistent with forty-day periods known to have been utilized in Egypt. In CH there is no mention of daily exorcisms as in ApTrad Ch. 20:3, indicating that this was not a practice in this com-

2. Stewart, *The Canons of Hippolytus*, 47–55.

3. Bausi, "The *Baptismal Ritual*."

4. For more on this, see Heinzgerd Brakmann, "ΒΑΠΤΙϹΜΑ ΑΙΝΕϹΕΩϹ: Ordines und Orationen kirchlicher Eingliederung in Alexandrien und Ägypten," in *"Neugeboren aus Wasser und Heiligem Geist,"* ed. Brakmann, Chronz, and Sode, 121–28 and 136–41; Nathan P. Chase, "Further Reflections on the Post-Baptismal Anointing and Handlaying in the Egyptian Tradition," in *Explorations in Christian Initiation from the East*, ed. Stefanos Alexopoulos, Nathan P. Chase, and Anna Adams Petrin, Eastern Catholic Studies and Texts (Washington, DC: The Catholic University of America Press, forthcoming).

munity. A *single* pre-baptismal, non-exorcistic scrutiny appears to be an Egyptian characteristic as well.[5]

An *apotaxis/syntaxis* unit has often been thought to be of Syrian origin or influence in Egypt, appearing also in the sacramentary of Sarapion of Thmuis, and the presence of an indicative baptismal formula is thought to be due to Syrian influence as well. In fact, because it is repeated three times, once each time with each of the three immersions, it appears likely to have been a recent interpolation or development. Further, as Bryan Spinks has shown,[6] baptismal rites known to the Cappadocian Fathers probably had only a *pre-baptismal* anointing. Hence, while the presence of a post-baptismal anointing in Egypt, as appearing in CH and the sacramentary of Sarapion, has often been seen as the result of Syrian influence,[7] it would be difficult to argue specifically for Cappadocia as its place of origin and/or influence. But Syrian influence in Egypt does not mean a Syrian and certainly

5. Maxwell E. Johnson, *The Rites of Christian Initiation: Their Evolution and Interpretation* (Collegeville, MN: Liturgical Press, 2007), 149–50. The recently published evidence from the Aksumite Collection largely confirms this. The scrutiny in BR-AC is tied to enrollment and is not exorcistic, though there is a reference to a healing "from evil to goodness." For the prayer, see Bausi, "The *Baptismal Ritual*," 65.11-21. The closest thing in Euch-AC is the prayer for those who are enrolled ($\Sigma50^{va}$–51ra) and for the laying on of hands on the catechumens in the block of independent intercessions ($\Sigma49^{ra}$).

6. Bryan D. Spinks, *Early and Medieval Rituals and Theologies of Baptism: From the New Testament to the Council of Trent*, Liturgy, Worship, and Society (Aldershot: Ashgate, 2006), 47–51.

7. See Gabriele Winkler, *Das armenische Initiationsrituale*, Orientalia Christiana Analecta 217 (Rome: Pontificio Istituto Orientale, 1982), *passim;* and Georg Kretschmar, "Beiträge zur Geschichte der Liturgie, insbesondere der Taufliturigie in Ägypten," *Jahrbuch für Liturgik und Hymnologie* 8 (1963): 1–54; here at 36 and 47–48.

not a Cappadocian provenance for CH. And, interestingly enough, the formula in CH is in the indicative rather than the passive voice.

Further, there is, of course, nothing Cappadocian about the threefold trinitarian creedal interrogation before baptism proper, now somewhat artificially connected to the three-times repeated baptismal formula. If anything, the threefold interrogation comes from ApTrad and so raises the question of the provenance of that document even more than it does for that of CH. An oddity of this creedal interrogation is the phrase "flowing from the Father and the Son," which has not received much attention. It was dealt with in passing by Hans Achelis,[8] Wilhelm Riedel,[9] and René-Georges Coquin,[10] but has been attended to in more detail by Stewart, who notes parallels to a number of fourth-century creeds and even possibly to a Caesarean formula.[11] He ultimately concludes "that the creed is not speaking of the eternal generation of the Spirit, but of the experience of the Spirit in the church."[12] What is clear is that this should not be interpreted as the Western filioque.

Stewart also argues that there is a lack of evidence for post-baptismal signings in the Egyptian tradition until later, but the BR-AC and the Euch-AC reference a full body pre-baptismal anointing[13] and an anointing of the forehead and

---

8. Hans Achelis, *Die ältesten Quellen des orientalischen Kirchenrechts 1: Die Canones Hippolyti* (Leipzig: Hinrichs, 1891), 217.

9. Wilhelm Riedel, *Die Kirchenrechtsquellen des Patriarchats Alexandrien* (Leipzig: A. Deichert, 1900), 212n4.

10. René-Georges Coquin, *Les Canons d'Hippolyte*, PO 31/32 (Paris: Firmin-Didot, 1966), 113.

11. Stewart, *The Canons of Hippolytus*, 52–53.

12. Stewart, 53.

13. Bausi, "The *Baptismal Ritual*," 69.23–71.21; Euch-AC: Σ52^{va}–52vb.

chest in the post-baptismal anointing,[14] both of which are closer to CH in their description than the Syrian parallels cited by Stewart. Stewart also argues against an Egyptian provenance since the post-baptismal prayer is not the same as that in Sarapion, but this only indicates it is not from Thmuis.

In his recent publication of Ethiopic I,[15] Alessandro Bausi has argued that the Greek text used by the Ethiopian redactor is fifth-century Alexandrian in provenance, and, hence, points to a strong Egyptian context, at least as the place where ApTrad may have been redacted and from where it was disseminated elsewhere. There is no reason, therefore, not to view the initiation materials in CH as reflecting, at least, a similar Egyptian redaction. But even more, as Bradshaw notes in a forthcoming essay: this would "open the door to the possibility that the original core of the baptismal rite in the *Apostolic Tradition* came from Egypt rather than North Africa."[16] Moreover, in §19e there is a parallel here to Dionysius of Alexandria's reference in *Ad Basileiden* 1 "that the paschal fast should not be concluded before midnight."[17]

14. Bausi, "The *Baptismal Ritual*" 79.17-22; not described in Euch-AC.

15. Bausi, "La 'nuova' versione."

16. Paul F. Bradshaw, "Fourth-Century Egyptian Baptismal Practice: A Reevaluation of the Evidence," in *Explorations in Christian Initiation from the East*, ed. Alexopoulos, Chase, and Petrin.

17. Stewart, *The Canons of Hippolytus*, 117n97. For the text, see Charles Lett Feltoe, ed., *St. Dionysius of Alexandria: Letters and Treatises* (London: Macmillan, 1918), 76–81.

CH §20

[20a] Concerning the Fast of Wednesday, of Friday, and of the Forty

The fast days which have been fixed are Wednesday, Friday, and the Forty. He who adds to this will receive a reward, and whoever diverges from it, except for illness, constraint, or necessity, transgresses the rule and disobeys God who fasted on our behalf.

[20b]

The bishop will send the catechumens bread purified by prayer, so that they may share in the fellowship of the Church.

The first part of this canon (20a) is a new creation in CH that does not appear in ApTrad, except in Ethiopic I where additional materials, including references to fasts on Wednesdays and Fridays, are inserted in-between ApTrad 43.1-3 and 43.4, making this additional material in Ethiopic I appear to be part of ApTrad, despite not being found in the other versions of the text. The material on fasting provides more concrete directives on fasting than what is seen in the other treatments of fasting in ApTrad and mirrors what is seen in CA 31 (Arabic), though it is also not as developed as what is seen in SD II.9-14 and 17 and V.1. At the same time, the reference in this canon to fasting on Wednesdays, Fridays, and the forty days, the latter of which Stewart translates as "Lent," is taken almost verbatim from Origen's *Homilies in Leviticus X.2*, where he says: "we have the forty days consecrated to fasting, we have the fourth and sixth days of the week, on which we fast solemnly."[1] Even if one wants to challenge the evidence provided by Origen's homily as belonging to the period when he was in Caesarea and not Alexandria, or because it may have been subject to emendation by his fourth-century Latin translator Rufinus, parallel references to both the Wednesday and Friday and the forty days fast appear in the canonical letter of Peter I of Alexandria.[2] In neither Origen nor Peter is there a particular reference to a liturgical context, with Peter's reference to an additional forty-day period attached to those undergoing penance. Even so, it points to Russo's comment that "quadragesimal fasting regimens [were] a hallmark of the early Alexandrian tradition.[3] And, as Bradshaw has noted in a recent essay:

---

1. Origen, *Homilies in Leviticus X.2*, W. A. Baehrens, GCS 29 (Berlin: Walter de Gruyter, 1920), 445.

2. Bradshaw, *The Canons of Hippolytus*, 25. See also Harald Buchinger, "On the Early History of Quadragesima. A new look at an old problem and some proposed solutions," in *Liturgies in East and West*, ed. Feulner, 99–117 [= *Studia Liturgica* 43 (2013) 321–41]; and Idem, "Origenes und die Quadragesima in Jerusalem. Ein Diskussionsbeitrag," *Adamantius* 13 (2007): 174–217.

3. Russo, *The Origins of Lent*, 389ff. See also Maxwell E. Johnson, "Liturgy in Early Christian Egypt," in Stefanos Alexopoulos, Harald Buchinger,

Thus, the most that can be said with any confidence is that the *Canons of Hippolytus* not surprisingly seem to reflect recommended practice in Egypt in the 330's [sic] when it has traditionally been believed to have been composed, prescinding from Alistair Stewart's recent claim that it is not Egyptian at all, but Cappadocian. The traditional date places it after Athanasius attempted to introduce a forty-day season of Lent at Alexandria immediately prior to Easter (as was also the case at Rome) and not terminating a week earlier as was usual in the East. Baptisms also seem to have been celebrated at the end of this forty-day season, but not linked directly to Easter. Instead, they were apparently on the sixth day of the sixth week, and when later the fast was moved back one week, the baptisms went with it, so that eventually baptisms were actually forbidden between Palm Sunday and Pentecost.[4]

It is worth noting that this canon is also almost exactly repeated in CA canon 31 (Arabic).[5] The last part of this canon (20b) is largely taken over from ApTrad 26.2 and 28.5 (for this reason also 29D), but with consideration, it seems, of ApTrad 27.1. There is, therefore, again nothing in this canon to suggest any other provenance than that of Egypt.

---

and Arsenius Mikhail, *Liturgies of the Church of Alexandria* (Washington, DC: Catholic University of America Press, forthcoming).

4. Bradshaw, "Fourth-Century Egyptian Baptismal Practice."

5. Riedel and Crum, *The Canons of Athanasius of Alexandria: The Arabic and Coptic Versions*, 31.

CH §21

[21a] Concerning the Assembly
of all the Priests and of the People
at the Church each Day

The presbyters are to assemble each day at the church, as will the deacons, the subdeacons, the readers, and all the people at the time when the cock crows. They are to perform the prayer, the psalms, the reading of Scripture, and the prayers, according to the precept of the Apostle who said, 'Apply yourself to the reading until I come.' He who does not hurry, but stays behind the clergy, except for illness, is to be excluded.

The major part of this canon, with the exception of the last part about the sick (21b, see below), pulls together all of the morning assemblies referenced in ApTrad 18, 19, 35, 39, and 41.[1] Morning assemblies were known throughout the ancient world, especially in Egyptian sources like Origen and GCN 2.1-4, 8.11-14, 14.2, and 15.5.[2] A morning assembly also appears in Egeria (381–384 CE), who is a witness to the fact that "the faithful continued to attend the daily *catechesis*, which lasted

1. Chase, "Another Look," especially p. 17.
2. Chase, 11–12.

for three hours after the morning office."[3] Ambrose of Milan (d. 397 CE) also expected Christians to go to church every morning to hear the Gospel.[4] Caesarius of Arles (d. 542 CE), too, appears to have known of a morning service with scripture readings and a sermon.[5] Whether the more catechetical services witnessed to by Egeria and perhaps others were the same as a morning service is unclear. But what we see is the widespread gathering of Christians in morning assemblies.

Bradshaw notes that this canon has a close affinity to Egyptian monastic *horaria* as evidenced by John Cassian, rather than non-Egyptian sources, which do not contain scripture readings.[6] Besides noting parallels here to GCN 6.5, Stewart also sees similarities to Pseudo-Athanasius's *De Virginitate* (fourth/fifth century, provenance unknown), which also references a virgin reading a book upon awaking if there is no church service.[7] Stewart notes that the parallel is "inexact,"[8] and in fact it is better paralleled in CH 27. More problematically, Stewart places *De Virginitate* in Cappadocia; however, the current scholarly consensus is that the provenance of the document cannot be determined.[9] As a

3. Paul F. Bradshaw, *Daily Prayer in the Early Church: A Study of the Origin and Early Development of the Divine Office* (New York: Oxford University Press, 1982), 90–91. Egeria, *Peregrinatio* 46.1–47.2.

4. Bradshaw, 112. Ambrose, *Expos. in Ps. 118, sermo* 19.32.

5. Bradshaw, 121–22. Caesarius, *Serm.* 72; 76.3; 86.5; 188.6; 196.2; 212.6.

6. Bradshaw, *The Canons of Hippolytus*, 26.

7. Stewart, *The Canons of Hippolytus*, 30–31.

8. Stewart, 31.

9. Stewart, 28. Here, Stewart relies on the work of Michel Aubineau, "Les écrits de saint Athanase sur la virginité," *Revue d'ascétique et de mystique* 31 (1955): 140–73. For a more recent treatment which leaves provenance open, see Teresa Shaw, "Pseudo-Athanasius: *Discourse on Salvation to a Virgin*," in *Religions of Late Antiquity in Practice*, ed. Richard Valantasis (Princeton, NJ: Princeton University Press, 2000), 82–99.

result, it is clear that the closest parallels to this canon in CH are to sources in Egypt.

[21b]

The sick will also find healing by going to the church to receive the water of prayer and the oil of prayer, unless the sick person is seriously ill and close to death. The clergy who know him shall visit him each day.

The latter part of canon 21 (i.e., 21b) on the sick is a new addition that has parallels in ApCons VIII.29 and the sacramentary of Sarapion Prayers 5 and 17, as noted by Bradshaw and Stewart, as well as the BR-AC and Euch-AC.[10] This additional material appears to place the healing ministry more firmly under the control of the clergy. Whether this oil was blessed with the oil in CH 3 is not clear. The text of that canon notes: "If there is any oil, he prays over it in this way, though not the same expressions, but the same meaning." The reference to the oil of prayer, seems to separate this oil from the oils used in the rites of initiation in CH 19c, namely the oil of exorcism and the oil of anointing (that is, the oil of thanksgiving). However, in the early period, there was not a clear distinction between various oils, particularly chrism/myron and oils for the sick.[11] A distinct oil for the sick was

10. Bradshaw, *The Canons of Hippolytus*, 26; Stewart, *The Canons of Hippolytus*, 60–61. For Sarapion, see Johnson, *The Prayers of Sarapion*. For BR-AC, see Bausi, "The *Baptismal Ritual*," 65–68 and 79–82. For Euch-AC, see Σ53^{vb}.

11. For an overview of the anointing of the sick, see Charles W. Gusmer, *And You Visited Me: Sacramental Ministry to the Sick and the Dying*, Studies in the Reformed Rites of the Catholic Church, vol. 6 (New York: Pueblo,

beginning to emerge, however, in this period. This was likely motivated by some tensions between Christian, medicinal, and magical uses of oil (see below).

What is perhaps more interesting is the reference to the sick to go to the church to receive the water and oil of prayer. The use of oil and water in Christian, medicinal, and magical contexts was common, especially in Egypt.[12] Each could be put on the body or ingested. The profuse use of oil and water in Christian and non-Christian rituals, magic in particular, led to tensions in the Egyptian church. This can be seen in the writings of Shenoute of Atripe,[13] who in a sermon

---

1984), Ch. 1. See also BR-AC (Bausi, "The *Baptismal Ritual*," 78/79–80/81) and Euch-AC (Σ53^{vb}–54ra). Pope Innocent I suggests that chrism was the oil used for the anointing of the sick; see Martin Connell, *Church and Worship in Fifth-Century Rome: The Letter of Innocent 1 to Decentius of Gubbio: Text with Introduction, Translation and Notes*, Joint Liturgical Studies 52 (Cambridge: Grove Books, 2002), 46–47. For the connection between oil and healing in the patristic period, see Béatrice Caseau, "Ordinary Objects in Christian Healing Sanctuaries," in *Objects in Context, Objects in Use: Material Spatiality in Late Antiquity*, ed. Luke Lavan, Ellen Swift, and Toon Putzeys, Late Antique Archaeology 5 (Leiden: Brill, 2007), 642 and 645–47; Korshi Dosoo, "Healing Traditions in Coptic Magical Texts," *Trends in Classics* 13 (2021): 44–94; Anne Grons, "The Question of the Effectiveness of Coptic Pharmacological Prescriptions," *Trends in Classics* 13 (2021): 129–30; Ágnes T. Mihálykó, "Healing in Christian Liturgy in Late Antique Egypt: Sources and Perspectives," *Trends in Classics* 13 (2021): 154–94.

12. Caseau, "Ordinary Objects"; AnneMarie Luijendijk, " 'If You Order That I Wash My Feet, Then Bring Me This Ticket': Encountering Saint Colluthus at Antinoë," in *Placing Ancient Texts: The Ritual and Rhetorical Use of Space*, ed. Mika Ahuvia and Alexander Kocar (Tübingen: Mohr Siebeck, 2019), 211–12; Grons, "The Question of the Effectiveness"; Mihálykó, "Healing in Christian Liturgy"; Dosoo, "Healing Traditions."

13. Dosoo, "Healing Traditions," 49–56.

(Acephalous Work A14) chastises those who seek healing oils and water from both magicians and the church:

> In the very moment of suffering, if they fall into poverty or a sickness, or indeed into other temptations, they renounce God and they rush to the feet of enchanters (*refmoute*) and oracles (*ma n-šine*) and do other deceitful deeds, just as I myself saw the head of a snake bound to the hands of certain men, and another with the tooth of a crocodile bound to his arm, another with the claws of a fox bound to his feet—and furthermore, it was a magistrate (*arkhōn*), who claimed to be wise! For indeed, when I reproached him, saying, "Is it the claws of a fox which will heal (*talkyo*) you?", he said to me, "It was a great monk who gave them to me, saying, 'Bind them to yourself and have relief' ". Listen to these impieties! Fox claws, snake heads, crocodile teeth, and so many other vanities in which men put their faith, saying that they will have relief because of them, while others are led astray by them. And again in this way they anoint (*tōhs*) themselves with oil, or they pour (*pōht*) water on themselves, having received it from enchanters or sorcerers (*refpahre*), together with every other type of deceitful relief. After they have said . . . again, they pour water on themselves, and they anoint themselves with water from the priest of the church, or indeed some monks. [. . .] If it is the oracles of demons that are of profit to you, and enchanters and sorcerers and all the other things of this type that do lawless things, indeed, go to their feet so that you will receive a curse on the earth. But if it is the house of God which is of profit to you, the Church, indeed, go there.[14]

14. Translation taken from Dosoo, 51–52.

This tension also appears in the CB canon 35 and a pseudo-Athanasian homily from the seventh or eighth century.[15] All of this likely also explains some of the references to the blessing of oil and water in CH, the prayers of Sarapion of Thmuis, BR-AC, and the exorcism of water for any purpose in the Euch-AC.[16] While there are some parallels to ApCons VIII.29, the weight of the evidence indicates Egypt.

15. Dosoo, 52–54.

16. For a summary of the evidence, see Mihálykó, "Healing in Christian Liturgy," 165, 170–71, 173, 176–80, and 187–88. For Euch-AC, see Σ54^{rb}.

CH §22

Concerning the Week of the Passover of the Jews, During which one sets aside Joy: concerning what one Eats then, and Concerning him who was Abroad and did not know the Pascha

<u>*During the week of the Passover of the Jews all the people are to take care with great vigilance to fast from every desire. One is not to say even a word with joy, but with sadness, knowing that the Lord of all, the impassible, suffered for us at this time, so that by [his] undergoing suffering we should escape the suffering which we deserve because of our sins. Let us also take a share in the suffering which he accepted for us, so as to have a share with him in his kingdom.*</u> *Food during the Pascha is bread and salt only, and water.*

If someone is ill or in a region where there are no Christians and the time of the Pascha ends without him having known its date, because of his sickness or owing to his solitude, these people are to fast after Pentecost and observe the Pascha with discipline. Let their intention be clear: they are not late through lack of reverence, and they do not fast in order to observe their own Pascha, or to establish another foundation than that which has been laid.

With the exception of the first paragraph, CH 22 is based on ApTrad 33. That this canon reflects an overall Egyptian redaction or context seems to be suggested by Stewart himself, who notes that the variant versions of the word *Pascha* employed here reflect "Coptic usage."[1] Stewart's argument for a Cappadocian provenance is based in part on what he considers to be theological parallels with the much earlier Asian-Quartodeciman Pascha.[2] The text in question is <u>underlined</u> above. In particular, Stewart sees the rationale for the paschal fast as based not on Alexandrian methods of calculation but Jewish and as sharing in the suffering of Christ to be indicative of a Quartodeciman context. But even if this focus may have been derived from a Quartodeciman source, which he does not provide beyond the unsubstantiated claim that it does, it seems to us highly speculative to claim that a mere reference to practices associated with the Jewish Passover indicates anything about adapting a Jewish paschal timetable or that imitating Christ in his passion is anything other than the influence of Romans 6 theology on the theology of Pascha, where rather than Christ being the sole protagonist of Pascha, the Christian now becomes a sharer in Christ's Passover.[3] Such a theological focus on participation is not to be viewed as only Quartodeciman but is as old as Origen of Alexandria's *Commentary on Romans* and comes to the fore universally in the fourth century, especially with the introduction of Paschal Baptism, a focus that would appear to concur with Stewart's mid-fourth-century dating for the CH as a whole (340–360 CE). Further, Stewart himself actually leaves the door open

1. Stewart, *The Canons of Hippolytus*, 121n105.
2. See Stewart, 4, 24–27, 35, 38, and 56.
3. See Raniero Cantalamessa, *Easter in the Early Church* (Collegeville, MN: Liturgical Press, 1993), 1–23.

here for Egyptian provenance in his statement that "even if the final collection is Egyptian its sources are not necessarily so."[4] But again, Cappadocian or other sources used in CH do not make CH itself Cappadocian. It might just make it non-Alexandrian, as Brakmann has argued based on CH 37.

4. Stewart, *The Canons of Hippolytus*, 35.

CH §§24/25a

[24] Concerning the Visit of the Bishop to the Sick: When a Sick Person has Prayed in Church and has a Home, he is to go there

A deacon is to accompany the bishop at all times to inform him of everyone's condition. He is to inform him about each sick person, because it is important for the sick person that the high-priest visit him. He is relieved of his sickness when the bishop goes to him, especially when he prays over him, because the shadow of Peter healed the sick, unless his lifespan is over. The sick are not to sleep in the dormitory, but rather the poor. That is why he who has a home, if he is sick, is not to be moved to the house of God. Rather he is only to pray and then return home.

[25a] Concerning [the Appointment of] the Steward of the Sick by the Bishop . . .

The steward is the one who has care of the sick. The bishop is to support them—even the vessel of clay necessary for the sick, the bishop is to give it to the steward.

Canon 24 and 25a will be treated together. Canon 24 is an adaptation of ApTrad 34 with possibly some remote influence from ApTrad 39, but Bradshaw has also noted parallels to CA canon 80 (Arabic).[1] The treatment in CH 25a on the institution of the steward of the sick is an adaptation of ApTrad 40.2—which in ApTrad was a cemetery steward—and parallels what can be seen in CA canon 80 (Arabic).[2] Stewart argues that the concern for the sick in CH points to a Cappadocian context, while having some parallels in the Egyptian tradition.[3] Part of his argument rests on the early witness to Christian hospitals for the sick and hospices for the poor (ξενοδοχεῖον) in Antioch and Cappadocia under the influence of Basil, and the fact that definitive Egyptian evidence for these institutions does not appear until the sixth century.[4]

While many scholars note that Basil provides the first definitive evidence of institutionalized hospices and hospitals, there is evidence for earlier charitable facilities that were less institutionalized and often tied to coenobitic monasticism,

1. Bradshaw, *The Canons of Hippolytus*, 27. Canon 80 is only partially extant in the Coptic. References to a "steward" also appear in CA canons 61 (Arabic and Coptic), 81 (Arabic and Coptic), 89 (Arabic and Coptic), and 90 (Arabic, not extant in Coptic); see Riedel and Crum, *The Canons of Athanasius of Alexandria: The Arabic and Coptic Versions*. For another look at the treatment of the sick in the CH, see Ric Barrett-Lennard, "The *Canons of Hippolytus* and Christian Concern with Illness, Health, and Healing," Journal of *Early Christian Studies* 13 (2005): 137–64.

2. Stewart, *The Canons of Hippolytus*, 60. Here Stewart means canon 80. Again, canon 80 is only partially extant in the Coptic.

3. Stewart, 7 and 38–41.

4. Peregrine Horden, "Poverty, Charity, and the Invention of the Hospital," in *The Oxford Handbook of Late Antiquity*, ed. Scott Fitzgerald Johnson (Oxford: Oxford University Press, 2012), 720 and 729–30.

particularly in Egypt.[5] Moreover, Stewart assumes that the κοιμητήριον described in CH is a formalized hospice like that established by Basil; however, the text does not seem to speak of a formalized institution and is quite vague as to what is being described. Additionally, support for the sick and poor were well known in non-monastic and monastic settings in Egypt, including the appointment of stewards.[6] There are also some parallels here to slightly later Egyptian healing centers, like that of Abū Mīnā and the martyrium of St. Colluthos, which contained places for incubations as well as houses.[7] This may indicate that something other than the Christian hospital and/or hospice is being described here. In fact, Shenoute in the passage above (see p. 61) seems to suggest a practice in the churches that mirrors what is described in this canon. Furthermore, CA in canons 14–15 (Arabic) make it clear that the bishop was charged with supporting and visiting the poor, orphaned, sick, and widows. In fact, the reference to "because the shadow of Peter healed the sick" in CH 24, which is taken over from Acts 5:15, is directly paralleled

5. Andrew T. Crislip, *From Monastery to Hospital: Christian Monasticism & the Transformation of Health Care in Late Antiquity* (Ann Arbor: University of Michigan Press, 2005), Ch. 4.

6. Wipszycka, "Les confreries," 513 and 516; Wipszycka, *Alexandrian Church*, for steward, see pp. 111, 114, 199, 256–58, for other support for the sick and poor, see Ch. 12.

7. Caseau, "Ordinary Objects"; Peter Grossmann, "Antinoopolis: The *Area* of St. Colluthos in the North Necropolis," in *Antinoupolis II*, ed. Rosario Pintaudi (Florence: Firenze University Press, 2014), 241–300. Priests sleeping in churches the week of holy Pascha is known from CA 57 (Arabic); see Riedel and Crum, *The Canons of Athanasius of Alexandria: The Arabic and Coptic Versions*, 38. This would seem to open the door for others routinely sleeping in churches.

in CA canon 14 (Arabic). In talking about the true bishop, that text states: "Whoso is occupied about the church, the people know that the shadow of his body healeth the sick."[8]

8. Riedel and Crum, *The Canons of Athanasius of Alexandria: The Arabic and Coptic Versions*, 26.

CH §§25b/26/27

[25b] [. . . Concerning the Times of Prayer]

Each person in the order of Christians is to pray when he rises from sleep in the morning—they are to wash their hands when they wish to pray, before doing anything. They are to pray again at the third hour, for it is the time when the Savior Jesus was voluntarily crucified for our salvation, so as to set us free. And again at the sixth hour they are to pray, because it is the time when all of creation shook because of the evil deed which the Jews did to him. At the ninth hour again they are to pray, because Christ prayed and surrendered his spirit into the hands of his Father at that time. And again at the time when the sun sets they are to pray, because it is the end of the day. When one lights the lamps in the evening, they are to pray, because David said, 'in the night I meditate.' And again in the middle of the night they are to pray because David also did that; and Paul and Silas, the servants of Christ, prayed in the middle of the night and praised God.

[26] Concerning the hearing of the Word in Church and Prayer There

When there is an assembly for the word of God in a church, everyone is to hurry and assemble there. They are to know that to hear the word of God is better for them than all the glory of this world. They are to reckon it a great loss to them when necessity prevents them from hearing the word of God. Rather, they should devote their time to the church frequently and [so] be able to expel hatred of their enemy, especially if someone can read, because it is more profitable to hear what one does not know. For the Lord, in the place where [his] majesty is remembered, makes the Spirit dwell in those who are assembled and gives his grace to all. Be reassured regarding those who are in two minds, because you have heard some of them in the Spirit. Those whose minds are preoccupied at home are not to forget what they have heard in church. That is why each one is to make it his concern to go to church every day when there are prayers.

[27] Concerning him who does not go to Church, Each Day he is to Read the Scriptures—Each Time you Pray, Wash your Hands—and Concerning the Exhortation to Prayer in the Middle of the Night and at the Time when the Cock Crows

Each day when there is no prayer in church, take a book and read from it. Let the sun see the book on your knees at each dawn.[1]

---

1. The word "book" here is translated as "Bible" in Bradshaw, *The Canons of Hippolytus*, 29, and "Scripture" in Stewart, *The Canons of Hippolytus*, 129.

The Christian is to wash his hands each time he prays. He who is bound by marriage is also to pray, even if he rises from beside his wife, because marriage is not impure and there is no need of a bath after second birth, except for the washing of the hands only, because the Holy Spirit marks the body of the believer and purifies him completely.

Everyone is to be concerned to pray with great vigilance in the middle of the night, because our fathers have said that at that hour all creation gives itself over to glorify God—all the ranks of angels and the souls of the righteous bless God. The Lord bears witness to this, saying, 'In the middle of the night there will be a cry: Lo, the bridegroom has come, come out to meet him.' At the time when the cock crows, again it is a time when there are prayers in the churches, for the Lord says, 'Watch, for you do not know at what time the master will come, in the evening, or in the middle of the night, or at cockcrow, or in the morning,' that is to say that we must remember God at each hour. And when one is lying on his bed, he must pray to God in his heart.

Let us do that, and instruct one another with the catechumens, in the service of God. The demons will not be able to sadden us, if we remember Christ at each hour.

These canons will be treated together and are largely based on ApTrad 41 (ApTrad 41 likely being a duplication and expansion of ApTrad 35).[2] While these canons revise the description of the hours as seen in the corresponding chapters in ApTrad and also rearrange their description, CH largely follows the same *horarium*, which appears as follows:[3]

---

2. Chase, "Another Look," 7–9 and 13.
3. Chase, "Another Look."

ApTrad 35 and 41	CH 25b–27
• Prayer at rising/cockcrow	• Prayer at rising
• A communal catechesis and prayer, or a private reading of "holy books"	• A morning assembly in the church or a private reading of books at cockcrow
• Prayer at the third hour	• Prayer at the third hour
• Prayer at the sixth hour	• Prayer at the sixth hour
• Prayer at the ninth hour	• Prayer at the ninth hour
• Prayer before bed	• Prayer in the evening/at lamp-lighting
• Prayer in the middle of the night	• Prayer in the middle of the night

The most significant departure is the fact that CH, unlike ApTrad, does not have a prayer at bedtime, instead having a prayer in the evening/at lamp-lighting.[4] It also seems to shift the reference to prayer at cockcrow from the prayer at rising as in ApTrad to the morning assembly.[5] Interestingly, CH also does not take over all of the Christological descriptions for the hours given in ApTrad 41.6-9. Furthermore, two rationales are given for prayer in the middle of the night. The first in canon 25b is based on the witness of David, Paul, and Silas. This is not paralleled in ApTrad 41. The second is in canon 27, which does parallel ApTrad 41.15-17. It appears that two traditions, one based on ApTrad and one based on a local tradition, are being brought together. This may explain the distinct canons in the text which largely duplicate one another.

As noted above with CH 21a, a reference to reading a book during the day appears in GCN 6.5 and Pseudo-Athanasius's

4. *Herm.Com.* 2002, 210.
5. Chase, "Another Look."

De Virginitate 20. There is, however, one interesting phrase in the canon not found in ApTrad: "Let the sun see the Bible on your knees at each dawn." Bradshaw notes that a similar line appears in Pseudo-Athanasius's *De Virginitate* 2 and the writings of Evagrius Ponticus,[6] though Stewart notes this is absent in the version of CH in the Berlin canonical collection.[7] With regard to CH 25b, Stewart cites some parallels to TD II.24 and Basil's *Regulae fusius tractatae* 37, and with regard to CH 26, he notes parallels to *The Epistle of Barnabas* 19.5a and ACO 13.2.[8] But there are also parallels in this section to GCN 6.5.[9] The parallels to Basil's defense of midnight prayer in his *Regulae fusius tractatae* 37 are all citations of scripture—Ps 119[118]:62 and Acts 16:25. With regard to CH 27, Stewart sees a similar concern for nocturnal prayer in *De Virginitate* 20, Basil's *Regulae fusius tractatae* 37, and TD I.22, I.32, I.42, II.19, and II.24.[10] But a concern for nocturnal prayer also appears throughout the Egyptian sources.[11] On the whole here, CH appears to be dependent on ApTrad, with parallels to Egypt, Syria, and Cappadocia; however, in looking at the sources, much of this material is scriptural, quite general in nature (like the attention to nocturnal prayer), or is derived from *formelgut*.

6. Bradshaw, *The Canons of Hippolytus*, 29.

7. Stewart, *The Canons of Hippolytus*, 129n124.

8. Stewart, 125 and 127. For the text of Basil's *Regulae fusius tractatae*, see PG 31:889-1052.

9. Stewart, 30–31.

10. Stewart, 43–44.

11. Robert Taft, *The Liturgy of the Hours in East and West: The Origins of the Divine Office and Its Meaning for Today* (Collegeville, MN: Liturgical Press, 1986), 63 and 65–66.

CH §28

None of the Faithful is to Taste Anything until after having Partaken of the Mysteries, especially on the Days of Fasting

None of the faithful is to taste anything until after having partaken of the mysteries, especially on the days of fasting.

The clergy are to see that they do not let anyone partake of the mysteries, except the faithful alone.

What was once descriptions for a home-communion service in ApTrad 36–37, have, according to Bradshaw and Stewart, become descriptions for the liturgy in the church in CH. Bradshaw marshals some evidence for communion services on fasting days in Egypt, namely Basil *Ep.* 93 and the possibility that a presanctified liturgy is instead implied.[1] Stewart disputes this and notes that TD I.22 and Basil *Ep.* 93 provide evidence for these days as days for a full eucharistic celebration, thus pointing away from an Egyptian context, since the evidence from Socrates's *Hist. Eccl.* 5.22 makes it clear the Eucharist was not celebrated on fasting days in

---

1. Bradshaw, *The Canons of Hippolytus*, 30.

Egypt.[2] However, Stewart's interpretation of Basil's *Ep.* 93 is incorrect—what is described is clearly the reception of communion, not a eucharistic service. Furthermore, the attribution of *Ep.* 93 to Basil has been disputed and it is instead attributed to Severus of Antioch (d. 538 CE).[3]

More importantly, there is Egyptian evidence, albeit in a monastic setting, that closely parallels what is described here.[4] Stefanos Alexopoulos in his work on the liturgy of the presanctified notes that in the fourth-century *Historia Monachorum in Aegypto* there is a daily communal liturgy that also included communion and was followed by a meal or other food (II.8 and VIII.50-51). There are also exhortations to daily communion (VIII.50-51), even as this is followed by a command to be attentive to the fasts (VIII.56-58).[5] While Bradshaw and Stewart see CH 28 as a liturgy, it may also still refer to a home-communion service, simply directing the clergy to ensure that the non-faithful do not receive the

2. Stewart, *The Canons of Hippolytus*, 131n131.

3. Robert Taft, "Home-Communion in the Late Antique East," in *Ars Liturgiae: Worship, Aesthetics, and Praxis; Essays in Honour of Nathan D. Mitchell*, ed. Clare V. Johnson (Chicago: Liturgy Training Publications, 2003), 17n8.

4. The prohibition to ensure that only the faithful receive the Eucharist would still make sense in a monastic setting, since many apparently entered the monastery un-baptized; see Hugo Lundhaug, "Baptism in the Monasteries of Upper Egypt: The Pachomian Corpus and the Writings of Shenoute," in *Ablution, Initiation, and Baptism: Late Antiquity, Early Judaism, and Early Christianity*, ed. David Hellholm et al. (Berlin: Walter de Gruyter, 2011), 1347–80.

5. Stefanos Alexopoulos, *The Presanctified Liturgy in the Byzantine Rite: A Comparative Analysis of Its Origins, Evolution, and Structural Components*, Liturgia Condenda 21 (Leuven: Peeters, 2009), 19–22. See also Robert Taft, *Beyond East and West: Problems in Liturgical Understanding*, 2nd ed. (Rome: Ed. Orientalia Christiana, 2001), 96–104.

Eucharist, something ApTrad and CH is concerned about throughout. At the same time, the parallels to a monastic setting should not be surprising since CH 38 contains material directed to ascetics.

CH §29

[29a] Concerning Vigilance over the Altar so that Nothing falls into the Cup: Nothing is to fall [into it] by [the fault of] the Priests or the Faithful, for Fear that an Evil Spirit should have Power over it. One is not to say anything behind the Veil, except in Prayer. When they have finished communicating the People, all those who enter into the [Holy] Place are to recite the Psalms in Place of the Bells. And Concerning the Sign of the Cross, and the Dust of the Sanctuary which is to be thrown into the Stream

The clergy are to stand with all their attention on the altar when it has been prepared. They are to stand watching over it, so that no insect climbs onto it and nothing falls into the cup, which would be a mortal sin for the presbyters. That is why everyone is to stand watching over the holy place. He who gives the mysteries and those who partake are to watch with great care that nothing falls on the ground, for fear that an evil spirit should have power over it.

[29b]

One is not to speak at all inside the veil, except prayer only and those things which are necessary for the service. One is not to do anything [else] in this place. After having finished communicating the people, they are to enter. They are to sing hymns each time they enter, because of the powers of the holy place. The psalms serve to replace the bells which were on the robe of Aaron. No one is to sit down in that place—only prayer, genuflection, and prostration before the altar.

The dust which is swept from the holy place is to be thrown into the water of a flowing stream, and one is not to delay for fear that it will be trodden on by people.

[29c]

Be pure at all times and mark your forehead with the sign of the cross, being victorious over Satan and glorifying in your faith. Moses did so with the blood of the lamb with which he smeared the lintels and the two doorposts, and it healed whoever lived there. How should the blood of Christ not better purify and protect those who believe in him and manifest the sign of salvation which is for all the world, which has been healed by the blood of the perfect lamb, Christ?

All the mysteries concerning life, resurrection, and the sacrifice, the Christians alone [are] those who hear them. This is because they have received the seal of baptism, in which they have participated.

The first part of this canon (29a) parallels ApTrad 37 and 38A. The material in 29b about veils, psalms, bells, and dust is new. The legislation regarding not speaking inside the veil parallels CB 96.[1] Bradshaw also notes parallels in the use of the veil in Athanasius's *Historia Arianorum* 56,[2] while Stewart notes correspondences with TD I.19 and 23.[3] Additionally, Stewart suggests some connection to ApCons VIII.12, but this remains very tangential.[4] The reference to the veils does not help in establishing the provenance of this section of CH since veils were used throughout the early Christian East[5] and we know that curtains adorned Egyptian churches.[6] Furthermore, CA canon 7 (Arabic) likely alludes to the use of a veil in the way that it compares the Christian church to the temple:

1. Bradshaw, *The Canons of Hippolytus*, 30; Stewart, *The Canons of Hippolytus*, 32 and 131.

2. Bradshaw, *The Canons of Hippolytus*, 30.

3. Stewart, *The Canons of Hippolytus*, 133n137.

4. Stewart, 133n136.

5. For a general overview, see Robin Jensen, "Altar Veils: Concealing or Displaying the Holy in Early Church Architecture," in *Why We Sing: Music, Word, and Liturgy in Early Christianity*, ed. Carl Johan Berglund, Barbara Crostini, and James Kelhoffer (Leiden: Brill, 2022), 409–32.

6. Elizabeth Bolman, "Veiling Sanctity in Christian Egypt: Visual and Spatial Solutions," in *Thresholds of the Sacred: Architectural, Art Historical, Liturgical, and Theological Perspectives on Religious Screens, East and West*, ed. Sharon E. J. Gerstel (Washington, DC: Dumbarton Oaks Research Library and Collection, 2006), 73–104; Béatrice Caseau, "Objects in Churches: The Testimony of Inventories," in *Objects in Context, Objects in Use*, ed. Lavan, Swift, and Putzeys, 562–67; Jennifer Ball, "Textiles: The Emergence of a Christian Identity in Cloth," in *The Routledge Handbook of Early Christian Art*, ed. Robin Jensen and Mark Ellison (Abingdon: Routledge, 2018), 224–29.

> If thou wouldst learn the truth, hear, that I may teach thee
> how thou mayest honor the church with all reverence. . . .
> Hear how God commanded Moses, 'Ordain for thy brother
> Aaron that he come not at all times within the veil before the
> altar, lest he die.' . . . And if He forbade Moses and Aaron,
> who did minister, to come within the veil at all times as they
> wished, how much the more them that with little reverence
> do talk in the holy place or that without shame dispute over
> the altar vessels or steal the first fruits of the altar?[7]

The reference to the psalms, bells, and dust is a new addition. A reference to psalm singing, though not in replacement for the bells, can be seen in CA.[8] A reference to the bells on Aaron's robe also appear in CA in the Arabic introduction and in canon 7 (Arabic).[9] The reference to dust being swept from the sanctuary is an interesting development, which must be an expansion of the concerns given in ApTrad 37 that nothing fall to the ground.

The description of the sign of the cross as being like the blood smeared on the doorposts in Egypt in 29c is taken over from ApTrad 38B and 42, the former being a doublet of the latter. The last line does not have a parallel in ApTrad, though there may be some correlation here to ApTrad 21.38-39.

7. Riedel and Crum, *The Canons of Athanasius of Alexandria: The Arabic and Coptic Versions*, 14.

8. Canon 49 (Arabic), Ibid., p. 36; canon 59 (Arabic and Coptic), Ibid., pp. 39 and 126; canon 78 (Arabic and Coptic), Ibid., pp. 49 and 136; and canon 92 (Arabic), Ibid., pp. 58–59.

9. Ibid., p. 4 and pp. 15–16, respectively.

CH §30

Concerning the Catechumens

The catechumens are to hear the word concerning the faith and teaching only. It is the judgment of which John speaks: 'No one knows it except he who receives it.'

On Sunday, at the time of the liturgy, if the bishop is able, he is to communicate all the people from his hand.

If a presbyter is sick, the deacon is to take the mysteries to him, and the presbyter is to take [them] himself.

This canon is an adaptation of ApTrad 21.40, 22, and 24 (=29B). Stewart has noted parallels here to the citation of Rev 2:17 in ApTrad 21 and CB 106, and he uses this to argue for the misplacement of certain sections in CH.[1] Stewart also thinks the material in this canon, rooted in ApTrad 22, was "originally relating to the carrying of the *fermentum*" in Rome and has instead been "adapted to deal with the issue of whether a deacon should give communion to a presbyter."[2] His read of ApTrad 22 is based on his own work on the document, in which he has argued that ApTrad is a third-century Roman

1. Stewart, *The Canons of Hippolytus*, 12–13.
2. Stewart, 15 and 135n146.

document.[3] There is no reason to see this as a description of the *fermentum;* rather, this is about the proper minister for the distribution of communion. As such, it reveals nothing about provenance.

3. Stewart, *On the Apostolic Tradition*, 157–61.

CH §32

Concerning the Virgins and Widows: They are to Fast and Pray in the Church. The Clergy are to Fast according to their Choice. The Bishop is not to be held to the Fast, except with the Clergy. And concerning a Meal or Supper arranged for the Poor

The virgins and the widows are to fast often and pray in the church. The clergy are to fast according to their discretion and their ability. The bishop is not to be held to the fast, unless the clergy fast with him.

If someone wants to make an offering and there is not a presbyter present in the church, the deacon is to replace him in everything, except for the offering of the great sacrifice alone and the prayer.

If one gives an offering to be given as alms to the poor, it is to be distributed before sunset to the poor of the people. But if there is more than is needed, it should be distributed the next day, and if anything still remains, on the third day. Nothing is to be credited to the donor alone. He is not to receive [anything], because the bread of the poor remained in his house by his negligence.

If there is a meal or supper made by someone for the poor—it is [a supper] of the Lord. The bishop is to be present at the time

> *when a lamp is lit. The deacon is to light it, and the bishop is to pray over them and over him who has invited them. It is right that he do for the poor the thanksgiving at the beginning of the liturgy so that they can be dismissed in order that they can depart before dark, and they are to recite psalms before their departure.*

This canon has thoroughly reworked the source material from ApTrad, in particular ApTrad 23; 24 (=29B); 25 (=29C). As Bradshaw notes, what was once a "community supper" in ApTrad has now "become a meal given by an individual for the poor."[1] Further light has been shed on this by Ethiopic I, which appears to preserve the original form of 29B.[2] Stewart thinks that this rather confusing section can be better understood based on Ethiopic I and TD II.11,[3] and he draws a connection to GCN 15.7 on the first fruits.[4] However, this chapter was clearly derived from chapters in ApTrad that once dealt with the Eucharist. Given the use of material from ApTrad in both this canon and the next few, Stewart rightly notes it is too difficult to determine provenance.[5] The legislation on clerical fasting also does not help determine provenance, though detailed descriptions for clerical fasting appear throughout CA.

The reference to the deacon taking over the offerings in the absence of a presbyter likely refers to something like the blessing of the first fruits in CH 3 and 36. CH 3, for instance,

1. Bradshaw, *The Canons of Hippolytus*, 32.

2. *Herm. Com.* 2002, 155. Here it appears to be paralleling CA §15 (Arabic), 36 (Arabic), and 47 (Arabic and Coptic).

3. Stewart, *The Canons of Hippolytus*, 137n150. See also pp. 58–59.

4. Stewart, 31.

5. Stewart, 59.

states: "If there is any oil, he prays over it in this way, though not the same expressions, but the same meaning. If there are any first fruits, anything edible, which someone has brought, he prays over it, and in his prayer, blesses the fruit which is brought to him." This rubric appears to conflate ApTrad 6 with 31 and 32. Part of these offerings were for the eucharistic celebration, which is likely why the text says the deacon may do everything "except for the offering of the great sacrifice alone and the prayer." The other portions were given for the sick, poor, widows, and even the clergy, which is probably why it has been included in this canon.[6] This is also confirmed by the prayer in CH 36 (see below).

6. For a summary, see Andrew McGowan, *Ascetic Eucharists: Food and Drink in Early Christian Ritual Meals* (Oxford: Clarendon Press, 1999), 89 and 127. However, this is also implied in the connection between the Eucharist and meal practices and distributions for the poor, sick, widows, and clergy in other sources. We can see connections between the support of the poor and other groups and the eucharistic celebration in Ignatius of Antioch (even if this may be shifting toward charitable meals; see Alistair C. Stewart, *Breaking Bread: The Emergence of Eucharist and Agape in Early Christian Communities* [Grand Rapids, MI: William B. Eerdmans, 2023], 71) and Clement of Alexandria (Stewart, 94–99), as well as later sources. The *Didascalia* 2.27.3-4, 2.28.1-2, 2.36.4, and 2.57.6, links the Eucharist and meals to the support of the poor, widows, and clergy, Stewart, 103–5. The ACO links the Eucharist and the poor, as well as clergy; see Stewart, 107–8. ApTrad 29B and 30A also address the material support of the widows, sick and the poor and were likely at one point eucharistic; see Stewart, 94–99. In addition to this canon in CH, this also appears in CH 34 and 35, which again may have also been, or at one point were, eucharistic; see Stewart, 100–102. GCN Ch. 15.7 links the giving of the first fruits and offerings to the Eucharist, which in the larger context of Ch. 15 seems to suggest outreach to the poor and those in need; see Stewart, *The Gnomai*, 83. In CA, the first fruits and offerings given to the clergy within the context of the Eucharist (Arabic and Coptic canon 63) are distributed to the clergy and for church use, as well as being distributed to the poor, widows,

As Wipszycka notes, in Egypt "offerings were handed over to deacons to be carried in a procession of gifts in the church and then divided up, primarily among the clergy. A part of foodstuffs was consumed immediately, during a meal held in the church complex, and whatever remained the clergy took home with them."[7] Theophilus of Alexandria also notes a meal after the Eucharist to receive leftover offerings: "The remainder of what has been offered for the sacrifice, when what is needed for the Mysteries has been consumed, is to be shared out by the clergy. But not even catechumens should eat and drink of these, only clerics and the faithful brethren with them."[8] This is largely repeated in CA 63 (Arabic and Coptic).[9] Canons 32 (Arabic), 33 (Arabic), 49 (Arabic and Coptic), and 50 (Arabic and Coptic) of CA also seem to indicate the celebration of a meal after the eucharistic celebration, but it seems that these are only for the clergy.[10] A communal meal in the church by the clergy is also described in canons 66–67 (Arabic).[11] Whether CA is attesting to multiple types of meals held in the church complex—some only for clergy

---

and sick by the bishop or his steward (Arabic canons: 3, 14–16, 61, 65, 69, and 82; Coptic canons: 47, 61, 62, 65, and 87); see Riedel and Crum, *The Canons of Athanasius of Alexandria: The Arabic and Coptic Versions*.

7. Wipszycka, *Alexandrian Church*, 202. See also Ewa Wipszycka, *Les ressources et les activités économiques des églises en Égypte du IVe au VIIIe siècle* (Brussels: Fondation Égyptologique Reine Élisabeth, 1972), 64–92.

8. Norman Russell, *Theophilus of Alexandria*, The Early Church Fathers (London: Routledge, 2007), 87. PG 65, 41.

9. Riedel and Crum, *The Canons of Athanasius of Alexandria: The Arabic and Coptic Versions*, 42 and 129.

10. Riedel and Crum, 32, 36, and 122–23. For more, see Wipszycka, *Alexandrian Church*, 401–3; Wipszycka, "A Certain Bishop," 102–3.

11. Riedel and Crum, *The Canons of Athanasius of Alexandria: The Arabic and Coptic Versions*, 43.

and some for all the faithful—seems likely. CH most certainly does attest to meals for the faithful. Perhaps this might point to an Egyptian context for this section of the canon.

The material from "If there is a meal or supper made by someone for the poor . . . they are to recite psalms before their departure" may indicate that the Eucharist was celebrated still directly within the context of a communal meal.[12] Stewart notes that the canon can be interpreted in two different ways, depending on how "the statement that the thanksgiving should be said first" is interpreted:

> There have been attempts to understand this as a statement that the meal is to begin with a eucharist since the word translated 'liturgy' above (*quddās*) is that generally employed in the Canons of Hippolytus for the eucharistic liturgy. Thus the phrase could mean either that he is to conduct the eucharistic liturgy at the beginning of the meal, or that he is to say certain words as a grace, which may possibly be the same words found at the opening of the eucharistic liturgy.[13]

Ultimately, Stewart concludes that "in this context it more probably refers to a grace before the meal; the canon is stating that the grace should use the same words as those used at the opening of the eucharistic liturgy."[14] The evidence from Theophilus of Alexandria and CA given above may provide some compelling reasons to see this as actually referring to a Eucharist celebration within a communal meal. This would also be consistent with the way that Stewart interprets Ap-Trad 29C, from which this canon is, in part, derived. In his

12. For the various ways of interpreting this passage, see Stewart, *Breaking Bread*, 100–102.

13. Stewart, 102.

14. Stewart, 102.

interpretation of ApTrad 29C Stewart has argued that there was a distinction between the eucharistic bread shared before the meal by the faithful and the non-eucharistic bread at the meal.[15] This interpretation has, however, been disputed by Bradshaw.[16] In any event, the redactor of CH does not include the note that "this is not the Eucharist" as contained in ApTrad 29C. This is either because it was clear to those who were using that text that it was not the Eucharist, or in fact it was still understood as eucharistic. Here CH may be preserving an older reading of ApTrad 29C than the received witnesses of ApTrad.

It is also worth mentioning that the references to distributing alms to the poor before sunset, as well as the need for the poor to depart before dark if there is a communal meal, is rather perplexing. The only parallel in ApTrad is to a similar practice for widows in 30A.1, which appears in CH 35. This must have had some practical explanation; however, the instruction is especially odd since the supper is prepared for the poor but parts of the community appear to stay after the poor are dismissed from their own supper.

The reference to the recitation of psalms parallels what is seen in ApTrad 29C.11-15, which appears in Ethiopic II and TD II.11, but not in Ethiopic I. It is unclear which represents the original form of the text.[17]

15. Stewart, 190.
16. Bradshaw, *Apostolic Tradition*, 90–91.
17. Bradshaw, 88–89.

CH §35

Concerning a Deacon present at a Meal in the Absence of a Presbyter. He is to replace him for the Prayer and the Breaking of the Bread, for the Blessing but not for the Body. Concerning the Dismissal of the Widows before Evening

A deacon at a meal in the absence of a presbyter is to replace the presbyter for the prayer over the bread. He is to break it and give it to the guests. With regard to the layman, it is not given to him to make the sign over the bread but to break it only, if there is no cleric there.

Each one is to eat what they have brought with every thanksgiving in the name of the Lord, so that the Gentiles may see your conduct and envy you.

When someone wishes to feed widows, he is to feed them and send them away before sunset. If they are numerous, lest they should be excited and not manage to depart before evening, he is to give each of them enough to eat and drink, and they are to depart before night comes.

In addition to reworking part of ApTrad 28 (v. 5-6) (=29D), this canon also adapts ApTrad 29A and 30A. Stewart notes a parallel in practice here to *Didascalia* 2.28.1,[1] but the material here in CH is taken over from ApTrad. Like in the previous canon, here the deacon is able to take over some responsibilities of the presbyter. There appear to be fewer restrictions here, though, except for the laity, presumably because there was no confusion with the Eucharist, though the practice described seems quasi-eucharistic. The alms given in canon 32 were also likely distributed to widows according to this canon. Furthermore, as noted in the discussion of the canon above (canon 32), the reference to the widows being able to depart before night must have some practical function.

---

1. Stewart, *The Canons of Hippolytus*, 145n163.

CH §36

Concerning the First Fruits of the Earth, the First of their Floors and their Presses: Oil, Honey, Milk, Wool, and the Rest which one brings to the Bishop for him to Bless It

Whoever has the first fruits of the earth is to bring them to the church, the first of their floors and the first of their presses, oil, honey, milk, wool, and the first of the produce of the work of their hands, all this they are to bring to the bishop, as well as the first of their trees. The priest who takes them is to give thanks to God for them, first outside the veil, while the one who has brought them remains standing. The priest says:

'We give thanks to you, Lord, almighty God, because you have made us worthy to see these fruits which the earth has produced this year. Bless, Lord, the crown of the year of your bounty. May they satisfy the poor of your people. Bless from your holy heaven your servant N., who has brought these things which are yours, because he fears you; bless him and all his house, and pour upon him your holy mercy, that he may know your will in everything, and cause him to inherit heavenly things; through our Lord Jesus Christ, your dear Son, and the Holy Spirit, to the ages of ages. Amen.'

Every vegetable, all the fruits of the trees, and all the fruits of the cucumber fields are to be blessed, and [also] him who brings them, with a blessing.

This canon is quite different from anything seen in Ap-Trad, though the closest parallels are to ApTrad 31–32. The prayer given in the text is totally different from the one given in ApTrad 31, though it is similar to TD II.16. However, the closest parallel is to MARK:[1]

CH	**MARK**
Bless, Lord, the crown of the year which is of your bounty, and may they satisfy the poor of your people.	Bless, Lord, the crown of the year of your goodness, for the poor of your people . . .[1]
Your servant *N.*, who has brought these things which are yours, because he fears you, bless him from your holy heaven, and all his house, and pour upon him your holy mercy . . .	. . . we set before you from your own gifts; and we pray and beseech you, for you are good and love humanity, send out from your holy height, from your prepared dwelling place, from your unbounded bosom, the Paraclete himself, the Holy Spirit . . .[2]

1. Bradshaw, *The Canons of Hippolytus*, 34; Stewart, *The Canons of Hippolytus*, 35–36 and 145n165. Chart adapted from Stewart, 35.

1. Johnson, *The Prayers of Sarapion*, 109.

2. Paul F. Bradshaw and Maxwell E. Johnson, eds., *Prayers of the Eucharist: Early and Reformed*, 4th ed. (Collegeville, MN: Liturgical Press, 2019), 114.

There is, therefore, a very strong Egyptian connection here, though the reference to "the crown of the year" is lacking in the earliest versions MARK (the Strasbourg Papyrus and in the version of MARK in Euch-AC),[3] as are the references to the Holy Spirit being sent from "holy heaven" and "his house," though the latter phraseology appears in other early Egyptian anaphoras.[4]

As noted above in CH 32, these first fruits were given for both the eucharistic celebration and the distribution to the poor, widows, sick, and clergy in the community. This is even explicitly mentioned in the prayer text: "May they satisfy the poor of your people." While the title attributes this blessing to the bishop, reference is made to the priest who receives the first fruits. This is another indication of the equality of the bishop and presbyters, but it also likely is an attempt to continue the ecclesiological principle that all alms are ultimately under the authority of the bishop and those appointed by him to manage them in his stead. This is something seen throughout CA.

3. See respectively, Bradshaw and Johnson, *Prayers of the Eucharist*, 89; Fritsch, "Two Ancient." For an edition of the text of MARK in the Euch-AC, see Polidori, *Alexandria Unveiled*, 112–18.

4. Chase, *The Anaphoral Tradition*, 224–25.

CH §37

Concerning the Fact that Every Time the Bishop offers the Mysteries, the Deacons and the Presbyters are to join [him], Clothed in White Garments, more magnificent than [those of] all the People: Similarly, the Readers

Every time the bishop offers the mysteries, the deacons and the presbyters are to join him, clothed in white garments, more magnificent than [those of] all the people, and [they are to be] more luminous still by their good deeds than [by their] garments.

The readers are also to be magnificent like them. They are to stand in the place of reading and are to succeed one another until all the people have assembled, and then the bishop is to pray and complete the liturgy.

This canon has no precedent in ApTrad. The issue with this canon comes, in large part, from the phrase "every time the bishop offers the mysteries." This, Brakmann notes, would be logistically impossible every week in places like Alexandria and

Oxyrhynchus that had multiple parishes.[1] He also connects this canon with CH 30;[2] however, canon 30 is addressing what should be done when the bishop is present at the liturgy, rather than insisting there is a single liturgy celebrated each week by the bishop. Furthermore, one could read CH 37 as saying that when the bishop celebrates the mysteries those presbyters and deacons who are present should celebrate with him. Brakmann and Stewart argue that the practice of the bishop gathering with his presbyters has no correspondence to Alexandrian tradition, with Stewart instead insisting that this points to an Antiochene context.[3] Brakmann, however, still argues for an Egyptian provenance for CH, but notes that it could not reflect the practice of a city with multiple parishes like Alexandria. While this practice may be odd in Alexandria, the gathering of a bishop and his presbyters is described in CA 28, 66, and 68 (Arabic and Coptic), as well as Athanasius's *Historia Arianorum* 60, Sozomen, *Historia Ecclesiastica* 2.22, and CB 96 and 97.[4] It might well be that these canons point to an Egyptian context outside of Alexandria or to a more exceptional gathering.

This canon may also point to an uncomfortable relationship between the liturgy of the Word and the eucharistic liturgy, since it appears that the readers read the readings as the assembly gathers. It is known from CA canons 49 and 50

---

1. Heinzgerd Brakmann, "Alexandreia und die Kanones des Hippolyt," *Jahrbuch für Antike und Christentum* 22 (1979): 139–49, especially p. 145. Further context can be seen in Wipszycka, *Alexandrian Church*.

2. Brakmann, "Alexandreia," 145–46.

3. Brakmann, "Alexandreia"; Stewart, *The Canons of Hippolytus*, 36–37, 41, and 42.

4. Bradshaw, *The Canons of Hippolytus*, 34. Bradshaw does not note parallels to CA 66 and 68.

(Arabic and Coptic) that priests were known to come in and out of the liturgy. Canon 50, for instance, says:

> If a priest come before the lesson and he be but seen and thereafter goeth forth to his work until the time of the offering come, the same shall not be given a portion; yet shall he be present at the eating. But if the necessity of his trade hinder his presence, he shall receive a portion, but shall tell the priest ere he depart. None shall take upon him this name, that is the priesthood, and despise it, but rather he shall perform his service even as all the Levites.[5]

That these two dimensions of the liturgy still had an uncomfortable relationship in some places into the fifth century is also clear from other sources. Reinhard Meßner has argued that the liturgy of the word was slow to be adopted into regular eucharistic practice in East Syria, something that is likely indicated in the Synod of Seleucia-Ctesiphon canon 13, which seeks to imitate the service in the West: "From now on we want to celebrate [the Eucharist] in the same way. Accordingly, the deacons in all the cities should proclaim the proclamation [i.e., scripture]. This is how the scriptures should be read. The pure holy sacrifice is to be offered on an altar in all churches."[6]

5. Riedel and Crum, *The Canons of Athanasius of Alexandria: The Arabic and Coptic Versions*, 36.

6. Oscar Braun, *Das Buch der Synhados oder Synodicon orientale: Die Sammlung der Nestorianischen Konzilien, zusammengestellt im neunten Jahrhundert. Nach der Syrischen Handschrift, Museo Borgiano 82, der Vatikanischen Bibliothek übersetzt und erläutert, mit kritischen und historischen Anmerkungen, Namen- und Sachregistern* (reprint Amsterdam: Philo Press, 1975), 21.

CH §38

Concerning the Night when our Lord
was Raised: No one is to Sleep that Night,
and one is to Bathe [beforehand]. Concerning
him who sins after Baptism and Explanation
of that, And the Prohibition of what one
ought not [to do], and of the Practice
of what one ought [to do]

As for the night of the resurrection of our Lord, one is to take great care that absolutely no one sleeps until morning. They are to wash their bodies with water before celebrating the Pascha, and all the people should be illuminated, because at this hour the Savior made all creation free and subdued heaven and earth and all that is in them, because he rose from the dead, ascended into heaven, and is seated at the right hand of God. He will come in the glory of his Father and of his angels, and he will reward each according to his deeds, those who have done good [with the] resurrection of life, and those who have done evil [with the] resurrection of condemnation, as it is written. That is why it is necessary that we are vigilant at all times, and that we do not give our eye to sleep or our eyelids to slumber until we find a place for the Lord.

Let no one say, 'I have been baptized and received the body of the Lord,' and feel confident and say, 'I am a Christian,' and then be stricken with love of things which he desires, heedless *of the commandments of Christ. Such a one as this is like one who enters the baths covered with dirt and comes out without rubbing himself, his dirt still on him, for he has not received the burning of the Spirit. As the blessed Apostle says, 'We burn with the Spirit.' All who have a mind that is not vigilant, it will be consumed, that is to say not alive in goodness, but dead in desires. They are balls, that is to say, a game for Satan to play with. For in the beginning they said with their lips, 'We reject you, Satan,' and now they hasten towards him with their evil deeds. INDEED, YOU DO NOT FIND SATAN AS HAPPY WITH THOSE WHO ARE WITH HIM AND COUNTED AS HIS AS HE IS WITH THOSE WHO ARE WITH US IN THE FLESH BUT WITH HIM IN SPIRIT, concerning whom the Apostle said, 'They declare that they know God and renounce him by their deeds.' It is said concerning them in Proverbs, 'As a dog returns to its own vomit, so is the ignorant man in his evil when he returns to his sins.' Blessed Peter says concerning them, 'They are like a sow that baths and then rolls in its mud.' It is no small sin that one should say before God, 'I will do all your will,' and decide also to serve Satan in disgusting desires, like a soldier who formally agrees to be a soldier but has no concern for military equipment or uniform. He would be exposed, even if he calls himself a soldier, because he has no uniform, but is only called a soldier as a formality. <u>So it is with one who says of himself that he is a Christian, but does not put on the deeds. He is called a devil by God and men, because he does not hate the deeds of the devils, but rather flourishes in them.</u> Therefore they receive the name due to them here and the fate due to them in the other place. The Savior says to them on that day, 'Depart from me, accursed ones, into the everlasting fire prepared for Satan and his angels,' for just as they loved his deeds on earth and remained associated with him in their life, so they will be in hell if they die in their unclean desires.*

For the Christian must walk in the commands of Christ, resembling God like beloved children, resembling Christ in everything. HE IS NOT ABUSIVE. HE IS NOT AN ADULTERER, OR SCORN-

FUL, OR A SCANDALMONGER. HE DOES NOT ACCUSE PEOPLE OF VAIN THINGS, NOR IS HE A DECEIVER. HE DOES NOT DESIRE PERISHABLE THINGS. HE IS NOT OBSTINATE, OR A LOVER OF GAIN, OR DISDAINFUL OF ANYONE. HE SHOULD NOT BE A GRUMBLER, OR PLAY THE JUDGE IN THE AFFAIRS OF OTHERS. HE SHOULD NOT SPEND HIS INHERITANCE ON THINGS IN WHICH THERE IS NO SALVATION, OR DO THAT WHICH SHOULD NOT BE DONE. HE SHOULD NOT BE UNMERCIFUL, OR BEAR FALSE WITNESS, OR LOVE TO BE SHOWN HONOR, OR BE GIVEN TO SCOLDING, OR BE A DRUNKARD OR A GLUTTON OR A LOVER OF THE WORLD OR A LOVER OF WOMEN; RATHER, HE SHOULD MARRY ONE WOMAN. HE SHOULD NOT BE ENVIOUS, OR SLACK IN CHURCH ATTENDANCE. HE SHOULD BRING UP HIS CHILDREN IN THE FEAR OF GOD AND NOT FLEE FROM TEMPTATIONS. HE SHOULD READ AND MEDITATE ON WHAT HE HEARS AND BE CONTENT. HE SHOULD NOT BE OPPRESSIVE OR QUICK TO GIVE A BEATING. RATHER, HE SHOULD QUICKLY PAY ANYTHING HE OWES LEST THE NAME OF GOD BE CURSED. HE SHOULD NOT BE LAZY, OR FORGET THOSE IN NEED WHO ASK HIM FOR HELP. HE SHOULD NOT DIVULGE SECRETS, OR CHANGE BOUNDARIES. HE SHOULD NOT BE A USURER, BUT RATHER A LOVER OF STRANGERS. HE SHOULD NOT DEAL CONTEMPTUOUSLY WITH HIS SLAVES, BUT COUNT THEM AS HIS CHILDREN. HE SHOULD NOT BE DIFFICULT IN GIVING AND RECEIVING, and should not have two scales or two measures. He should not be slow to bring offerings and the first fruits. He should have no dealings with the Gentiles, or mix with them. HE SHOULD BE A WORKER IN THE SERVICE OF GOD, NOT DEPARTING FROM THE COMMANDS OF THE GOSPEL OF GOD, WHICH HAS BEEN PROCLAIMED TO ALL OF CREATION UNDER THE HEAVENS.

If the Christian is firmly established in all this, that is, resembles Christ, he will be at his right hand, and be sent with the angels and receive honor from him, because he has obtained the beautiful crown, fulfilled the charge, kept the faith, and will receive the crown of life which was promised to those who love him.

If the Christian wishes to be in an angelic rank, let him keep away from women completely and decide in his heart not to look at them or eat with them. Let him quickly distribute all his accumulated possessions to the weak and impose on himself the rule of the angels in humility of heart and body. Let him support himself and be like the birds that have no tools. Let him give to the poor from [what he earns] with the work of his hands, [with] offerings and much prayer and much fasting. LET HIM KEEP HIS FAMILY AWAY AND BEAR ALL THE SUFFERING THAT COMES TO HIM FOR THE SAKE OF GOD. Let him carry his cross and follow the Savior and be ready to die at any moment for the sake of Christ, in faith.

For it is inevitable that the man who seeks perfection should be tempted as our Lord Jesus was tempted by those three temptations—gluttony, pride, and love of gold. For the tempter turned his attention to our Savior when he was fasting and said to him, 'If you are the Son of God, say that these stones should become bread.' AND YOU TOO, O ASCETIC, YOU FAST VOLUNTARILY, BY YOUR OWN INTENTION. **Do not accept his thoughts, for he will persuade you to break your customs, especially if it is a fast of religion. Rather, reply to your thoughts and say like your master that man does not live by bread alone, but by every word that proceeds from the mouth of God.**

THE SAYING, 'THAT THESE STONES SHOULD BECOME BREAD,' HAS ANOTHER INTERPRETATION, FOR HE MISLEADS THOSE WHO LOVE POSSESSIONS AND CAUSES THEM TO TELL THE STONES TO BECOME POSSESSIONS, AND THEY LOVE POSSESSIONS, [WHETHER THEY BE] STONES OR SAND, AND HE MAKES THEM THINK THAT THEY WILL LIVE BY THEM, LIKE BREAD, SO THAT THE WORD OF THE LORD MAY BE REMEMBERED THAT SAYS THAT IF ONE'S POSSESSIONS INCREASE HE WILL NOT FIND HIS LIFE IN THEM. **Therefore, love not money, you lovers of God, for the root of all evil is the love of money, and let your mind be without care. It is said, 'We have food and clothing, let us be content** *with that.' But hear the words of blessed David when he says, 'Cast your care on the Lord and he will support you,' especially since the Apostle Peter says, 'Cast all your cares on him for he cares for you.'*

When the evil one sees that a man's faith is such as this, the second temptation comes to him, for he sets him on a pinnacle of the temple, which is perfection in the virtues, and [tries to] persuade his heart to reject them all; [this is the meaning of] 'throw yourself down from here.' He tells him, 'virtue is hard and you will not be able to endure this suffering for the whole earth.' He does not allow him to think of the Savior, who said, 'Have no care for tomorrow.' FOR WHOEVER RAISES HIMSELF UP BY VIRTUE, IT IS SAID THAT HE IS BROUGHT BY SATAN TO THE HOLY CITY, BUT THEY DO NOT REMAIN [THERE] BECAUSE THEY HAVE NOT ACQUIRED VIRTUES FOR GOD BUT RATHER FOR THE SAKE OF VAINGLORY. This is [the meaning of] the serpent saying, 'so that they may be honored by men.' So they throw themselves down from the pinnacle of the temple and are split open internally and what is inside them comes out and they are more empty than they were at the beginning.

Therefore, in the hour when a man makes a covenant before God and worships him, let him be firmly on his guard lest he fall. It is written, 'God is not mocked,' and 'God is not to be tempted.' If a man is not vigilant and does not constantly remember God at every hour, he falls into the worship of idols, WITHOUT KNOWING THAT THE WORSHIP OF IDOLS IS ONLY THAT A MAN SHOULD THINK THAT HE ALONE IS CHOSEN AND THAT HE IS BETTER THAN EVERYONE ELSE. This is the pride that is unclean in God's reckoning. If Satan persuades someone that he is better than anyone else, it is this that constitutes his falling down and worshipping him, because he does not know the word that the Lord said, 'I am meek and humble of heart,' and he does not understand the saying, 'You worship the Lord your God alone

<u>*and serve him.' Therefore, beloved, flee from the worship of idols, which is pride.*</u>

Let us love one another, love strangers, and love knowledge; let us flee from every evil partner and hasten towards the servants of God and devote ourselves to serve [God] with them. For Abigail said to David, 'This is your servant, ready to be a servant to you, to wash the feet of those who serve you,' in order that we too should wash the feet of the saints. Let us listen to him who is greater than David, Jesus Christ, our Lord, your blessed model. He will respond to everyone who keeps his commandments well, 'O good and faithful servant, you have been faithful over a little. I am setting you over much. Enter into the joy of your Lord.' He truly says to each of us gathered in his name, 'Come, O blessed of my Father. Inherit the kingdom prepared for you before the foundation of the world. I was hungry and you fed me. I was thirsty and you gave me drink. I was a stranger and you gave me shelter. I was naked and you clothed me. I was sick and you visited me. I was a prisoner and you attended to me.' He spoke, and the righteous replied and said, 'O Lord, when did we see you hungry and feed you, and so on?' And he answered and said, 'Truly, I say to you, as you did it for one of these little brothers, so it was for me that you did it.'

Whoever keeps these canons, the peace of the Lord be upon him, and mercy upon the whole Israel of God. The enemy will find no rest in them. Rather, they will find rest with all the pure ones in the kingdom of our Lord Jesus Christ, through whom be glory to the Father and the Holy Spirit, to the ages of ages. Amen.

The apostolic Canons of St. Hippolytus, Archbishop of Rome, are completed in the peace of the Lord, to whom be thanks and glory always. Amen.

This is a totally new creation in CH; however, the start of the canon in its reference to washing before the paschal vigil parallels what is seen for those being baptized in ApTrad 20.5 and even CH 19, as does the reference to not sleeping that night (ApTrad 20.9 and CH 19). But there are also parallels to other sources. There are "some similarities . . . to the interpretation of the temptations of Christ" in the work of Evagrius Ponticus (**bolded** above), as well as John Cassian and Pseudo-Athanasius's *De Virginitate* 7, 8, and 22 (both are <u>underlined</u> together above).[1] Stewart also notes some possible terminological parallels to the "Two Ways" (text in SMALL CAPS above above) and one clear parallel to GCN 1.11-12 <u>double underlined</u> above. He also suggests more broadly that this canon functions like the framing material in *Fides partum* (fourth century, Egypt) and the SD.[2] Similar framing, and even content, also appears in Ethio-MC 1–12, particularly 7–8.

Based on the parallels to Pseudo-Athanasius's *De Virgini-tate* and the writings of Evagrius, Stewart suggests an Asian origin for this canon, which he argues comes from homiletic material directed toward an ascetic:

> It would not be unreasonable to suggest that *Can. Hipp.* 38 is drawing on a common fund, whether written or oral, circulating in the same area and period. However, we may also suggest that this common fund, and possibly even the homily on which *Can. Hipp.* 38 is based, is not Egyptian but, like *De virginitate* itself, Cappadocian. Such an impression of

1. Bradshaw, *The Canons of Hippolytus*, 37.

2. Stewart, *The Canons of Hippolytus*, 20–23, 27–30, 38, and references in the notes from pp. 153–59. For an overview of the *Fides*, see Alessandro Bausi, "La Versione Etiopica Della *Didascalia Dei 318 Niceni* Sulla Retta Fede e La Vita Monastica," in *Aegyptus Christiana: Mélanges d'hagiographie Égyptienne et Orientale Dédiés à La Mémoire Du P. Paul Devos Bollandiste*, ed. Ugo Zanetti and Enzo Lucchesi (Geneva, 2004), 225–48.

a common fund is strengthened if one were to note the other parallels observed by Coquin from the writings of Evagrius Ponticus and the *Sententiae* of Nicaea [GCN].[3]

He writes later that while the "Evagrian parallels might point to an Egyptian provenance, we must remember the Pontic origin of Evagrius, and his time spent with Basil and Gregory, and wonder whether *Can. Hipp.* 38, with its Evagrian echoes, in fact reflects an Asian asceticism being brought to Egypt, rather than a native Egyptian spirituality."[4]

There are a number of issues with this analysis by Stewart. To begin with, again, Pseudo-Athanasius's *De Virginitate* is not attributed by current scholars to Cappadocia. Furthermore, while it is true that Evagrius is from Pontus, this is a tenuous connection, and we know that Evagrian-type Origenism was a large problem in Egypt in the fourth and fifth centuries.[5] Furthermore, there are parallels here to Egyptian texts like GCN, *Fides*, and SD. Possible connections to the *Didache* are interesting and would not rule out an Egyptian context. The *Didache* was cited by early Egyptian writers, though only the "Two Ways" section of the document may have been intended.[6] Nevertheless, whether or not early Egyptian writers were referencing just the "Two Ways" section of the text or both the "Two Ways" and the liturgical portions of the document, phrases from *Didache* Chs. 9 and 10 appear

---

3. Stewart, *The Canons of Hippolytus*, 28.

4. Stewart, 30.

5. Elizabeth A. Clark, *The Origenist Controversy: The Cultural Construction of an Early Christian Debate* (Princeton, NJ: Princeton University Press, 1992), 156–57.

6. Kurt Niederwimmer argues that the liturgical sections quoted in Egyptian prayers are simply rooted in a common tradition; see Niederwimmer and Attridge, *The Didache*, 4–17.

as intertexts in early Egyptian eucharistic prayers.[7] This and other evidence strongly suggests that the liturgical parts of the *Didache* were also circulating in Egypt at an early date.[8]

Stewart does put forward another possibility for the origins of this canon:

> Coquin points out that the same treatment of the temptations of Christ is found in John Cassian *Conf.* 5. He concludes that the version in *Canones Hippolyti* is the least developed, however of the discussions, and is therefore most likely to be earliest. One cannot help but agree, in particular given the other evidence which indicates a date for *Canones Hippolyti* in the middle of the fourth century. The indications are either that *Canones Hippolyti* is a source for the Evagrian material or, given the linkage with *De virginitate*, that *Canones Hippolyti*, for all that it is a redactional composition, is drawing upon a forming ascetic tradition into which Evagrius had also tapped.[9]

7. Nathan P. Chase, "Shaping the Classical Anaphoras of the Fourth through Sixth Centuries," in *Further Issues in Eucharistic Praying in East and West*, ed. Maxwell E. Johnson (Collegeville, MN: Liturgical Press, 2023), 23–60.

8. See also Jonathan Schwiebert, *Knowledge and the Coming Kingdom: The Didache's Meal Ritual and Its Place in Early Christianity*, Library of New Testament Studies 373 (London: T&T Clark, 2008), Ch. 8. A few other pieces of evidence suggest this, mainly the changes made to *Didache* Ch. 10 in the Coptic fragment Br. Mus. Or. 9271 (Copt.) and the number of early Egyptian and Ethiopian sources; see Niederwimmer and Attridge, *The Didache*, 21–27. While not known to Niederwimmer and Attridge, fragments of the *Didache* appear in the Aksumite collection; see Alessandro Bausi, "La *Collezione Aksumita* Canonico-Liturgica," *Adamantius* 12 (2006): 43–70; Bausi, "La 'nuova' versione."

9. Stewart, *The Canons of Hippolytus*, 29.

This seems the more probable explanation. While it leaves provenance somewhat open, it does not point definitively to Cappadocia. In fact, it more probably points to Egypt based on parallels to contemporary texts like GCN, *Fides*, and SD, as well as Ethio-MC.

Conclusion

Having looked at the differences between ApTrad and CH, the evidence overwhelmingly indicates that CH was composed in Egypt and should be dated between 336–340 CE. Furthermore, this study suggests some overarching conclusions about CH:

- CH is a derivative of ApTrad that in some places may also attest to older readings of its source-text.

- The editor of CH attempted to make its source-text (ApTrad) usable for their community.

- All of the parallels between CH and Cappadocian sources have parallels in Egyptian sources as well, while the reverse is not true. This does not, as Stewart suggests, point to two redactions in the text; rather, it points to a single Egyptian redaction.

- CH cannot be much later than the mid-fourth century, as indicated by the treatment of ordination in the text. Given the dating of ApTrad, this further points away from two redactional layers in the text.

In line with the work of Brakmann and Stewart on CH, it is unlikely that CH emerged from Alexandria, though it clearly emerged somewhere within its orbit. Instead, CH reflects Egyptian practice in either the *chora*, Pentapolis/Cyrenaica, or possibly even further afield—Nubia cannot be discounted.

Finally, therefore, while questions of provenance are always difficult to answer, there is not enough evidence to replace or even challenge the traditional scholarly consensus that CH is both the earliest derivative of ApTrad and of Egyptian origin.